*Golfer*

------------------------------

*Season*

------------------------------

*Team/Club*

------------------------------

# The Golfer's Workbook

## – A Season of Golf & Reflection –

Richard Kent and Ken Martin

A companion book to

*Writing on the Bus: Using Athletic Team Notebooks and Journals to Advance Learning and Performance in Sports*

*Dedications...*

For the players of the annual Kent Open... my brothers Allen, Fred, Ken, and Rob... *RK*

For playing partners Hilary and Bill, JEE, and Niles—thanks for patient listening... *KM*

*Acknowledgements...* Thanks to those who provided feedback along the way: Suzie Cary, Staci Creech, Rob Kent, Hilary Martin, Todd McKinley, Niles Parker, Ken Trevett, and Torrey Viger.

*Front Cover Photo:* Portmarnock, Dublin. Robert E. Kent

Copyright © 2018 Richard Kent
Writing Athletes
National Writing Project
All rights reserved.
ISBN-10: 0986019194
ISBN-13: 978-0986019197

This book is published in cooperation with the National Writing Project, University of California, 2105 Bancroft Way, Berkeley, CA 94720

# Contents

Introduction..................................................................7

Pre-, Mid-, and Postseason Planning & Reflection..................17

Your Golfing Routines.....................................................29

Golfer's Journal & Playing Record......................................37

Practice Sessions..........................................................125

Health and Fitness........................................................157

Additional Writing Activities...........................................167

Appendix: Creating a Personal Par....................................171

Other Notes.................................................................173

About the Authors........................................................195

# Introduction

"Pay attention. Take notes. Write them down."
—Pia Nilsson & Lynn Marriott

This workbook can help you become a better, more satisfied golfer. You probably read golfing magazines, watch The Golf Channel, think about your game while driving to work, discuss your game with friends or an instructor.... But do you write? You should. Writing is a powerful tool for learning in any sport.

Listen to these few lines from *Writing to Learn* by William Zinsser on the value of writing in all arenas, from the business world to the classroom:

> Writing organizes and clarifies our thoughts. Writing is how we think our way into a subject and make it our own. Writing enables us to find out what we know—and what we don't know—about whatever we're trying to learn.

Elite athletes from Olympians to professional golfers analyze their practice sessions and games in training logs, notebooks, and journals. This writing helps them unpack their game and improve.

We've based *The Golfer's Workbook* on what we've discovered from these athletes. Writing is powerful, but it's neither complicated nor mysterious. We've designed activities that take just a few minutes to reflect and write after a match or a practice session. By putting energy into these activities, you will learn more about golf and about yourself as a player.

Writing in this book will not replace time spent on the practice range or course. You won't immediately add distance to your drive because you wrote about that pesky 12$^{th}$ hole. What this book can do is complement what you're already doing, or plan to do, to achieve your goals as a golfer.

And like all those other ways you build your game, writing takes persistent effort to make a difference. Writing muscles, like any muscles, get stronger with practice. So, if you've read the books, watched the videos, taken the lessons, practiced, played, and talked about your game and you're still not satisfied, writing could be the missing piece.

Nilsson and Marriott recommend keeping a journal of winning strategies. Writing itself can be one of those winning strategies. So let's get started.

*Self-Assessment Quick Write*

First, we'd like to ask you two questions: Why do you play golf? And, what are your hopes or aspirations for your own game?

Write for 3-5 minutes in the columns below. Don't worry about complete sentences or explanations. Just list your thoughts in fragments and phrases.

| Why do you play this game? | What are your hopes for your game? |
| --- | --- |
|  |  |

Now look at your lists. Did you write about fixing your swing and lowering your scores? Spending time outdoors with friends? Exercise? Competition?

Nilsson and Marriott identify five elements to golf:

- Physical (fitness, nutrition)
- Technical (grip, club fitting, shot-making)
- Mental (motivation, decision making)
- Emotional (temperament, reactions)
- Social (interactions with others)

How many items on your list fit into some or all of these categories? Go back to your lists on page 8 and mark the category each item falls into.

*The Golfer's Workbook* does not provide direct instruction on any of these five elements. Instead, we pick up where other books leave off by creating a space for you to process and learn from all those other teaching resources you use.

In *The Inner Game of Golf*, Tim Gallwey presents our golf experience as a balance of performance, enjoyment, and learning—the PEL triangle. Gallwey maintains that this triangle is too often lopsided in favor of performance at the expense of learning and enjoyment. He goes on to say,

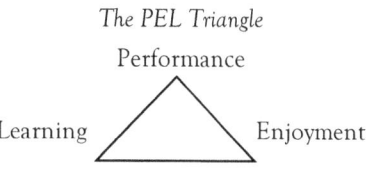

> The irony is that in the process of sacrificing all for the sake of performance, we sacrifice performance as well. Why? Because, over the long run, high-level performance requires continuous learning and is sustained by enjoyment.

Writing builds the learning side of your golf triangle directly. Activities in *The Golfer's Workbook* play across all five aspects of the game, from the physical to the social, helping to even out all three sides.

*Free Write: My Game in Balance*

In the space provided on page 10, write about a challenging or positive golf experience you have had. Describe what happened and then comment on what you did, what you learned, and what you enjoyed about this event. Ken gives an example in "My Day at the Beach" on page 11, using his story of one challenging hole at Riviera Country Club in Ormond Beach, Florida. Read "My Day at the Beach" and then write your own.

## Free Write: Your Golfing Triangle

Recall a golfing success or challenge:
- Describe the event.
- Write about what you did,
  what you learned, and what you enjoyed about the experience.

Don't worry about filling the page. Just write without stopping for 3-5 minutes.

Title: _____

> *My Day at the Beach*
>
> The 12th hole at Riviera is a 164-yard, par-3. My drive with a 5-hybrid soared into the prevailing wind and overcast sky and came down just 10 feet left of the pin. Sadly, it landed not on the green but plugged in a greenside bunker. After four chops at the wet, hard-packed sand, I finally popped my ball onto the grassy wall of this trap. My chip from there rolled 12 feet past the hole, and, adding irony to insult, I sunk that 12-foot putt coming back. Seven strokes on a par-3. Frustrated and embarrassed, all I wanted was to leave that hole behind. Later, writing helped me to see what had happened through the prism of the PEL triangle.
>
> *Performance: What I did...*Looking back, I realized that I did not consider the lie, and I let my club lose momentum in the wet, hard sand. More importantly, I stayed in the bunker, flailing at my ball in a hurry to fix the problem and not delay my playing partners.
>
> *Learning: What I could take away...*When I don't get out of a bunker, I need to *physically* get out of the bunker. I need to step out, take a breath, and make a fresh start to prevent the situation from spiraling out of control. I didn't do that. With each attempt, I got more tense and hurried, feeling guilty for holding others up. Alternate approach: To avoid a big number, lay up in front of the green to a much easier chip.
>
> *Enjoyment: What went well...*Looking back, I also realized that I'd actually hit a pretty good tee shot. Plus, I drained a putt for which bogey golfers like me have only about a 15% probability!

*Natural Learning in Golf*

*The Golfer's Workbook* is based on two principles shared across well-respected sports psychology resources listed on page 14. First, each of us is unique, so each of us should have a unique golf swing. Ultimately, you need to play your own game, and developing that game should be an ongoing source of enjoyment.

Second. Learning, especially learning a physical activity, is a natural process that begins with awareness. We act and respond to the results of our action: Hit an 8-iron in the water? Select the 7-iron next time out. But wait. Was it club selection or a sudden gust of wind? Or did my mind wander and I hit my ball anyway? The most obvious answer is not always the right answer. Broad awareness of what we do as well as the conditions that surround us is the linchpin that holds our action and response together.

Of course, we can all benefit from instruction, or reading and trying what's suggested in golf magazines. With or without instruction, one of the best ways to learn a physical skill is simply to play—not just in the sense of getting out on the course, but in the sense of exploring, experimenting, observing what happens, reflecting on what it can tell us, and then trying again.

What *The Golfer's Workbook* provides is a structure to support you in this natural learning process.

*Write. Learn. Perform.*

Golf has a long history with writing. We keep a running record during play. Professionals and caddies record as much information as possible about each course as well as the player's performance. Increasingly, we learn of players that routinely write in a journal—a practice recommended by golf instructors and sports psychologists.

Golf is uniquely suited for writing because there is ample time in-the-midst of play to record observations. And writing is especially important for recreational golfers. Before, during, and after play, we are player, caddy, swing coach, psychologist, agent, physical therapist, and more. Writing is a way to carry out these many different roles.

At Writing Athletes we have a guiding principle: Write. Learn. Perform. We know that writing is a proven way to capitalize on experience, draft a vision, and plan for the future. For those interested in steady, continuous improvement, writing increases awareness and deepens reflection.

Written reflection will also add to your enjoyment of the game. We all have a tendency to overemphasize poor outcomes. As you track your performance, you will be surprised at how often your game measures up; and other activities in this workbook will help you to recall the many reasons you play what Arnie called "the greatest game ever invented."

Of course, writing alone won't fix flawed swing mechanics, course management, or physical fitness. But it's less likely those areas will improve without writing. The plain fact is that writing amplifies learning, and it does so for young and old, new and experienced, proficient and developing. And, writing will almost certainly increase any player's enjoyment of the game by releasing negative energy and celebrating the positive (see sidebar).

> Physiological and Psychological Benefits of Writing:
> - reduces stress and anxiety
> - increases self-awareness
> - sharpens mental skills
> - promotes genuine psychological insight
> - advances creative inspiration and insight
> - strengthens coping abilities
>
>     - Stephanie Dowrick, Ph.D.

Bobby Jones said, "One reason golf is such an exasperating game is that a thing we learned is so easily forgotten, and we find ourselves struggling year after year with faults we had discovered and corrected time and again." One approach to overcoming that golf hazard is to write.

*How you might use* The Golfer's Workbook

There is no one right way to use this workbook. Page through the different sections and use each in a way that works best for you. We've provided a variety of prompts to stimulate your thinking and lots of space for writing.

For those interested in a roadmap, here's what we had in mind:

*Pre-, Mid-, and Post-Season Planning & Reflection* (p. 17) will help you to think a bit more about your interests and objectives. There are pages to reflect on your history as a golfer and on the ways you learn best. Then, there are pages to plan and reflect at the beginning, middle, and end of your season.

*Your Golfing Routines* (p. 29) are the foundation for your game. There is room to record and reconsider how you warm-up and what you do before and after individual shots as well as between shots and throughout a round.

*The Golfer's Journal & Playing Record* (p. 37) is the heart of this workbook. We hope you will use it throughout your season to write about individual rounds and other topics. After a separate introduction, there are playing record forms on each left-hand page to help you review your rounds and plan next steps. On each right-hand page there are suggestions for writing about different physical, mental, emotional, and social aspects of your game.

*Practice Sessions* (p. 125) is similar to the Journal. This section includes pages for planning and reviewing your time at the range, practice green, and elsewhere. There are also suggestions for thinking and writing about topics like club selection and expanding your arsenal of recovery shots.

*Health and Fitness* (p. 157) is a place to reflect on your readiness to play. About every 8-10 rounds, we recommend that you review hydration, nutrition, and sleep records to identify trends that support or interfere with your performance. You may also plan any cross-training activity (e.g., treadmill, weights) and consider any injuries you may be managing.

*Additional Writing Activities* (p. 167) includes 15 prompts for those who have fallen in love with writing. There's also space to describe your fantasy golf foursome and to plan your dream golfing trip.

*Other Notes* (p. 173) provides room for whatever doesn't fit anywhere else. This section includes some graph paper for sketching and planning strategy for holes you play or perhaps designing your own ideas for ideal golf holes.

*Other Tips on using this workbook*

What makes writing easier? Routine. Deciding when and where to reflect after each round will be especially important. An explanation of how to use the playing record forms in this workbook begins on page 38. Sooner will be more productive than later for these reflections, but find your own best time and stick to it. Other supports like a favorite pen or pencil and a cup of coffee can also help to trigger writing.

Protect your workbook but don't lock it away. You probably won't keep your workbook in your golf bag, but you may want to keep it in your kit bag, and we recommend a zip-lock bag to protect it from water and dirt. Try to keep your workbook handy to capture thoughts before they get away, especially after you come off the course following a round.

Quick Write. When responding to a prompt, try to write without stopping for 3-6 minutes. If your mind goes blank, make a list of words until you start writing sentences again. Just keep writing and the thoughts will come to you.

Just Write It. Don't be overly concerned with perfect writing. Don't stop to spell check or correct grammar or wonder if you've found just the right word. Write for an audience of one: You!

*Watch this seven-minute video on the home page of* WritingAthletes.com:

Before you dive into *The Golfer's Workbook*, we'd like you to hear from Maverick McNealy– Stanford University graduate and 2015 NCAA Player of the Year. In this Golf Channel interview, Maverick explains how writing helped him on his way to becoming a professional golfer.

## Recommended Reading

*Zen Golf: Mastering the Mental Game* by Dr. Joseph Parent

*The Inner Game of Golf* by W. Timothy Gallwey

*Golf Is Not a Game of Perfect* by Dr. Bob Rotella

*Every Shot Must Have a Purpose* by Pia Nilsson & Lynn Marriott

*Mastering Golf's Mental Game* by Dr. Michael T. Lardon

Notes:

# Pre-, Mid- and Postseason Planning & Reflection

The following pages will help you to think deeply about your golfing interests and objectives. You'll be prompted to reflect on your history as a golfer and the way you learn best. Use the pre-, mid-, and postseason pages at the beginning, middle, and end of your season.

## Your Timeline as a Golfer

Look back at your golfing career by creating a timeline. Include your golfing milestones like your first match, teacher, set of clubs; highlight special courses you've played, events and competitions, learning breakthroughs. List chronologically whatever reveals the important moments of your golfing life.

*Golfer's Timeline*

Write about one thing you noticed or thought about while filling out this timeline?

## Earliest Memory

Write about your earliest memories as a golfer.

# How Do You Learn?

We interviewed a number of athletes about how they learn in their sport. Look at this figure and circle the ways you learn as a golfer.

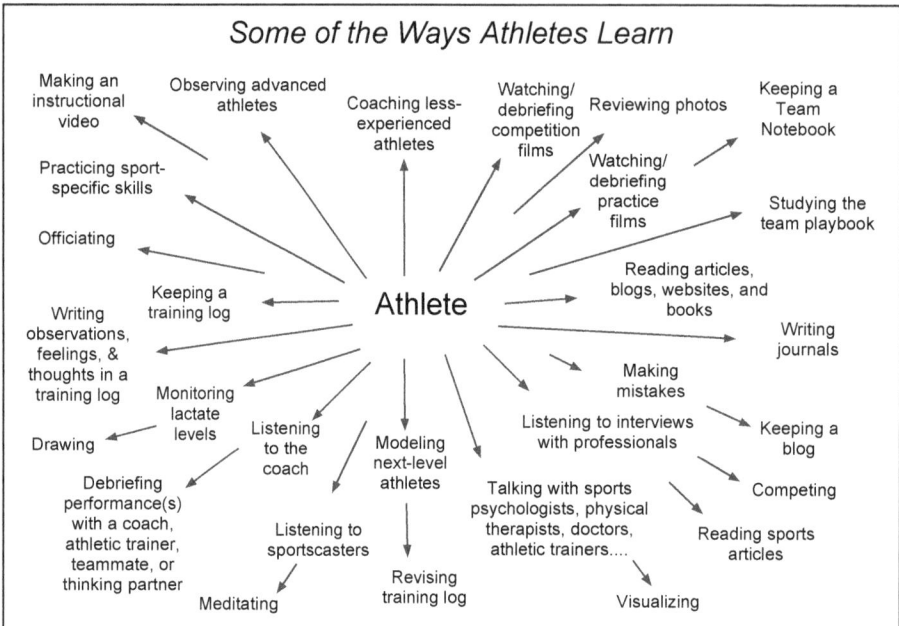

Reprinted with permission from *Writing on the Bus* (Kent, 2011, p. 14)

Looking at the various learning tools above, what could you add to your own practice and learning experience to help you improve at golf?

Are there ways you learn that are not included in the figure above? List them below.

Notes:

# Preseason Reflection & Planning

The prompts below will guide you in thinking back to your last golf season and ahead to the coming season. You'll return to this section at midseason and at the end of the season to reflect and revise your plans.

What were your strengths last season?

What interfered with achieving your goals for performance, learning, and enjoyment last season?

In the off-season, what did you do related to golf (e.g., reading and viewing, nutrition and health)?

Write about and describe a particularly satisfying golf outing from last season. What made this event stand out?

Write about a particularly disappointing golf outing from last season. What made this event stand out?

Identify your intentions for golf in the coming season. Be sure to include enjoyment and learning objectives as well as any performance goals. Also, be sure that each intention is specific, reasonable, and within your control. Add essential steps for pursuing each goal.

| What I intend to achieve this season. | How I plan to achieve these intentions. |
|---|---|
| | |

What are your practice session priorities for this season? List three priorities for how you will organize practice range or green activity and other training. Rather than listing results of training (those go above), identify actions within your control—for example, time spent, frequency, and how practice sessions will be structured.

1.

2.

3.

# Midseason Reflection & Planning

Use the following prompts to reflect on your game so far this season.

What are your strengths so far this season?

What has continued to challenge you this season?

Memorable Moments...Write about a particularly satisfying example from this season in each category.

Enjoyment

Learning

Performance

What are you most proud of so far this season?

Go back and review your preseason plans. Revise your original intentions and add any new objectives. Remember to consider enjoyment and learning as well as performance.

| My New & Revised Intentions | How I plan to achieve these intentions. |
|---|---|
| | |

Review your preseason priorities for practice sessions. Rank how you have done on each. Write a comment and revise your practice plans as needed.

| I can do better | A-Okay | Great | | |
|---|---|---|---|---|
| | | | 1 | |
| | | | 2 | |
| | | | 3 | |

# Postseason Reflection & Planning

Use the following prompts to reflect on your game this season.

What have been your strengths this season?

What continues to challenge you?

What has been your most significant accomplishment this season?

What are your plans for the offseason?

What are your practice session priorities for next season?

1.

2.

3.

# Postseason Letter

Write yourself a letter describing what you achieved this season and what you aspire to achieve for next season. Be sure to discuss all three legs of the triangle: enjoyment, learning, and performance.

*Try This:* Make notes here. Then write your letter on a separate piece of paper and seal it in a self-addressed, stamped envelope. Give the envelope to someone you trust and ask them to send it to you on a date shortly before next season starts.

Notes:

# Your Golfing Routines

Your routines are the foundation for your game. On the following pages you'll record and reconsider how you warm-up and what you do before and after individual shots. You'll also be prompted to think about your routines between shots and throughout a round.

# The Perfect Warm-up

Outline your ideal warm-up routine before a round. List each activity, the time it takes, and how the activity helps you prepare.

| Activity | Time | How it helps me prepare |
|---|---|---|
| | | |

*My Quick-Start Warm-up*

How do you warm-up when you arrive at the course without much time before teeing off (say, 15 minutes). What do you do, for how long, and why? What are you leaving out? How might this affect your performance and enjoyment? What changes to the quick-start could you try?

# Pre-shot Routine for Driving and Iron Play

"A sound pre-shot routine is the rod and staff of the golfer under pressure."

–Dr. Bob Rotella

Focus, concentration, and keeping self-interference at bay. Playing your best, most confident and comfortable golf requires commitment to a pre-shot routine that you trust. Outline your pre-shot routine from start to finish. Then, you might write about what each piece does for you, where it sometimes breaks down, changes you have thought about making, and so on.

Other stuff...what do you do when you are "between clubs"? What lies do you find easier or more challenging to play from?

# Pre-shot Routine for Reading and Making Putts

"Hitting a golf ball and putting have nothing in common. They're two different games."

— Ben Hogan

Outline your routine for reading and stroking putts. Then, you might write about how your routine helps you to make the transition from ball striking to putting. You might also identify what disrupts your routine and how you handle such disruptions.

More... Write about your most memorable putt, things you admire about others' putting (including the pros), reads or putts you find easier or more difficult.

# Post-shot Routine

"Find something good to say about every shot—or say nothing."

—Dr. Joseph Parent

Outline your post-shot routine starting from the end of your follow-through. How do you watch your shot? Record your shot? Respond to different kinds of results?

# Between Shots

How do you spend your time between shots (or between holes)? Do you think about your game, look around, or talk with others? Does your routine change as you get closer to the hole? Write about your routine between shots.

*Or Try This*: Write down what you really want when you play golf. Since most of our time during a round is spent not playing golf, how can this time contribute to achieving what you really want from the game?

# At the Turn

Transition from the ninth green to the tenth tee can be a dangerous time (Is that hot dog really the best choice?) or a helpful time. Write about what you do and say at the turn. Nutrition: What do you eat and drink? Performance: Do you total your score for the front nine? Reflect on how you are playing today and re-set intentions for the back nine? Enjoyment: How do you refresh and reenergize?

*Mini-turns*: Many golfers divide their round into three-hole segments and re-set after each.

Notes:

# Golfer's Journal & Playing Record

This section is the heart of the workbook. Use these Playing Records and journal prompts to write about individual rounds and other topics throughout the season. After the introduction, there are 40 Playing Records that will help you think deeply about your rounds and plan next steps. Opposite the Playing Records are writing prompts focused on physical, mental, emotional, and social aspects of your game. And remember: Write. Learn. Perform.

# Playing Records and Your Personal Par

In *Zen Golf: Mastering the Mental Game*, Dr. Joseph Parent calls par "an illusory 'box' that mid- to high-handicap golfers create for themselves." Seventy-five percent of golfers average *at least* one shot above par on each hole (see sidebar).

For most of us recreational and developing golfers, measuring against scratch par sets us up to fail; and scorecards and signs at each tee, screaming the course par, exacerbate the problem.

What Parent recommends is changing whatever par is printed on scorecards to match both your own average score and the current course and conditions, "...making it your 'personal par for the day.'" Parent goes on to say

> You will become much more at ease approaching a difficult hole from this perspective. It will also encourage more patience in recovering from a mis-hit, knowing you have that extra stroke or two to get to the green.
>
> You'll also feel much better at the end of a hole... instead of dejectedly saying, "I made another double-bogey," you get to say, "I made my par!"

*Golf: It's tougher than we think!*

Percent of golfers and their average score according to the National Golf Foundation:

- 5% Under 80
- 21% 80-89
- 29% 90-99
- 24% 100-109
- 10% 110-119
- 11% 120+

Not only will this shift increase your confidence and enjoyment from the round, but also as Parent suggests, this brighter mindset can be the foundation for better play.

The playing records in this workbook support this approach. The top includes space to record course information and conditions as well as your readiness to play and warm-up. Then, the following steps explain how to review your round and plan future activity.

*Step 1*: Set your personal par for the course.

In golf, a handicap is the number of strokes a player may expect to score above par based on averaging a number of the golfer's rounds of play. For many, a USGA handicap will provide this benchmark. If you don't have an official handicap, the Appendix explains how to work out an unofficial number as well as how to modify a handicap for different courses.

At his home course, Ken's handicap is 18, which he adds to the scorecard par of 70 for a total of 88: Home course scorecard par  70  plus handicap  18  equals  88 , Ken's personal par for the course.

*Try it*: Your course scorecard par \_\_\_\_ plus your handicap \_\_\_\_ equals \_\_\_\_, your personal par total for a round of 18 holes.

*Step 2*: Assign your individual par to each hole.

This step is easy if your par is exactly 18 (or 36): Simply add one (or two) shots to the scorecard par on each hole. Otherwise, you will want to adjust some holes by increasing or decreasing extra strokes. For example, if your par total is 22 (i.e., 18 plus 4), you will select four holes to which you add two rather than one stroke; and if your par total is 15 (18 minus 3), you will select three holes for which you use the scorecard par without adding any strokes at all.

This may seem confusing at first. Just focus on the goal of setting a realistic number for each hole based on how you ordinarily score. Your playing records should help you decide which holes to adjust. Add extra strokes to holes you find most challenging, and subtract strokes from holes you find easiest to play. (The Appendix also explains the USGA way to decide where to add or subtract strokes.)

*Try it*: The Table shows how Ken distributes his personal par across nine holes at his home course. Take a few minutes and record the scorecard par at a course you play and assign your own personal par numbers in this table:

| Hole | 1 | 2 | 3 | 4 | 5 | 6 | 7 | 8 | 9 | Total |
|---|---|---|---|---|---|---|---|---|---|---|
| Ken's course scorecard par | 4 | 3 | 5 | 3 | 3 | 4 | 4 | 4 | 5 | 35 |
| Ken's personal par | 5 | 4 | 6 | 4 | 4 | 5 | 5 | 5 | 6 | 44 |
| Your course scorecard par | | | | | | | | | | |
| Your personal par | | | | | | | | | | |

*Step 3*: Review your results.

Continuous improvement depends on reflection after each round—more than just sharing highlights over a beer with playing partners. Replaying your round in writing will magnify the learning you take away, and it should also be encouraging and joyful.

Our brains naturally remember out-of-the-ordinary events, both good and bad. We recall those 40-foot putts holed and 8-irons over water to within four feet of the pin; but we tend to emphasize missed opportunities and failed attempts more, and steady play is apt to fade from memory altogether. The detailed evidence of a written reflection reminds us of how consistently we moved the ball forward and into the hole. And planning to keep this record will sharpen your attention and observation on the course. Pages 40-42 provide a complete example and explanation for using *The Golfer's Workbook* playing record.

# How to Use the Golfer's Playing Record

*The Header*
- Record basic details: date, course name (location) and other information (course and slope ratings and green or cart fees), your start and end times, and other players and the event, if any.
- Describe your readiness to play: hours of sleep the night before or how well rested you felt; and your hydration and nutrition intake before and during the round.
- Note weather conditions including any changes during the round.
- Describe your warm-up.

Over time, these details will identify patterns that help or interfere with your performance.

*The Box Score*

Space is provided to record results of your round.
- Yardage for each hole and, rather than recording the scorecard par for each hole, record "My Par": What you consider your personal par number for each hole.
- Actual Scoring:
  - Strokes: Record your number of strokes taken at each hole. You may also want to mark a ✓ or an "F" in the strokes box where your drive landed in the fairway.
  - Putts: Putting makes up 40-50% of any golfer's game. It's important to set benchmarks and track this part of your game separately. You may also want to mark a ✓ or a "G" for any "greens in regulation" according to your personal par.
  - These figures allow you to total fairways hit and GIR (greens-in-regulation) as well as total strokes and putts for your round.
- Plus/Minus (+/−): Make a check-mark (✓) when your actual strokes-taken matches your personal par for a hole. When you take more strokes than your par, note "+" and the number of added strokes (e.g., "+1" on hole #1); when you take fewer strokes than your personal par, note "−" and the number of strokes (e.g., "−1" on hole #4). This notation makes it easy to see where you are gaining and losing strokes against your personal par.

*Performance Observations*

You might ask yourself, "Where am I gaining and losing strokes?" and use what the numbers reveal to guide comments and next step recommendations to yourself. Here, along with an overall summary of performance, I celebrate good putting, and I unpack some disappointing bunker play and "take away" a next step for overcoming this challenge.

*Other Reflections*

There's no sharp line separating performance observations and other reflections, but this is space for whatever you want to write or take away from the round. Try to observe before you interpret—that is, put what happened into words before speculating on what it means.

(Continued on page 42)

# Playing Record

Date __May 20__   Course __Meadow View__

(Walk)/Ride   Time Start __8:15__ End __12:45__   Course Rating __66.4__   Slope __113__ Fees __$30__

Players/event: __Saturday Sunrise League – Mark S (12), Kevin (16), Boomer (22)__

Sleep __7 ½ hours__   Hydration before __16 oz. water__   During __16 oz. water__

Nutrition before __OJ, toast, eggs (2), coffee (8 oz).__   During __PBJ, carrots, orange, granola__

Weather __65°, lite wind (3-4 mph), mist turned to rain by #16__

Warm-up __Quick Start. Basic stretching. No range. Putting green 5 minutes__

| Hole | Yards | My Par | Actual Strokes/Putts | | +/- |
|---|---|---|---|---|---|
| 1 | 453 | 6 | 7 | G3 | +1 |
| 2 | 153 | 4 | 5 | 2 | +1 |
| 3 | 317 | 5 | 5 | 1 | ✓ |
| 4 | 370 | 5 | F 4 | G1 | -1 |
| 5 | 398 | 5 | F 5 | 1 | ✓ |
| 6 | 187 | 4 | 5 | G3 | +1 |
| 7 | 505 | 6 | 7 | 2 | +1 |
| 8 | 147 | 4 | 4 | 1 | ✓ |
| 9 | 315 | 5 | 5 | G2 | ✓ |
| Out | | 44 | 47 | 16 | +3 |
| 10 | 323 | 5 | 4 | G2 | -1 |
| 11 | 415 | 5 | 5 | 1 | ✓ |
| 12 | 164 | 4 | 6 | 1 | +2 |
| 13 | 485 | 6 | F 6 | G2 | ✓ |
| 14 | 405 | 5 | F 5 | G2 | ✓ |
| 15 | 127 | 4 | 4 | G3 | ✓ |
| 16 | 390 | 5 | F 6 | 1 | +1 |
| 17 | 480 | 6 | 5 | G1 | -1 |
| 18 | 370 | 5 | 6 | 2 | +1 |
| In | | 45 | 47 | 15 | +2 |
| Total | | 89 | 94 | 31 | +5 |

Fairways: __5__   GIR: __9__   Total: 94 / 31 putts

## Performance Observations

1. Scoring Summary:
- 11 of 18 holes: made or bettered my personal par.
- Good day on the greens: Averaged fewer than 2 putts per hole (1.72)
  - 8 1-putts over the round were helped by 4 bump-&-run from just off the green
  - 91 feet of holed putts including 12' – 15' – 12' – 14' on the back 9.

2. Performance issue of the day: "6" strokes on #12! ☹

My 5 hybrid landed hole high and within 10 feet left of the pin, BUT in the greenside bunker. It took 4 strokes to get out—unlike holes #2 & 8 where I escaped traps on my first try.

Looking back, I realize the sand was wet and hard by the afternoon, and I let the blade dig in and lose momentum. Take away: Study up on handling that kind of lie. But don't lose confidence in your bunker play!!

## Other Reflections

I spotted an oriole in one of the protected areas. Boomer brought his homemade granola mix for everyone.

> "Preparation for the next round begins in the way we review the round we have just finished."
>
> —Pia Nilsson & Lynn Marriott

Above all, stay positive with your reflections, accentuating where you met or bettered your plans. *Ways to Reflect on Results* (below) lists different ways to do this.

Don't overlook the memorable things that happen—who you played with, wildlife you noticed on the course, something funny, beautiful...

During a winter get-away to Florida, Ken played with four French-Canadian snowbirds from Montreal and learned a lot about finding retirement real estate in the Daytona Beach. During another round at Victoria Hills in DeLand, he was accompanied all day by sandhill cranes, a protected species so numerous they have their own road crossings at this course. People and the world outdoors—two reasons worth recalling for why we love and play this game.

---

*Ways to Reflect on Results*

Use these to vary how you look at your rounds. Note how the emphasis throughout is on strengths to build on and other positives.

- Lessons Learned and Next Steps.
- Good, Better, How: What was good about my game today? What could I do better? How can I improve on those aspects of my game where I need to do better? (Nilsson & Marriott)
- Memorable Moments: Describe one moment you want to keep for future reference. Describe one moment you'd like to do-over and explain how. Describe one moment that was just plain fun.
- Write about the "arc" of your round. How did your focus, fun, confidence, style of play, etc. change or develop over the round?
- How did your routine(s) support you today? What happened that surprised you? What key decisions did you make today? How hard did you work today?
- How was your self-talk or your talk with others (positive, negative, thoughtful)?

Notes:

# Playing Record

Date_____Course_____

Walk/Ride   Time Start_____End_____   Course Rating_____Slope_____Fees_____

Players/event: _____

Sleep_____Hydration before_____During_____

Nutrition before_____During_____

Weather_____

Warm-up_____

| Hole | Yards | My Par | Actual Strokes/Putts | +/- |
|------|-------|--------|----------------------|-----|
| 1    |       |        |                      |     |
| 2    |       |        |                      |     |
| 3    |       |        |                      |     |
| 4    |       |        |                      |     |
| 5    |       |        |                      |     |
| 6    |       |        |                      |     |
| 7    |       |        |                      |     |
| 8    |       |        |                      |     |
| 9    |       |        |                      |     |
| Out  |       |        |                      |     |
| 10   |       |        |                      |     |
| 11   |       |        |                      |     |
| 12   |       |        |                      |     |
| 13   |       |        |                      |     |
| 14   |       |        |                      |     |
| 15   |       |        |                      |     |
| 16   |       |        |                      |     |
| 17   |       |        |                      |     |
| 18   |       |        |                      |     |
| In   |       |        |                      |     |
| Total|       |        |                      |     |

Performance Observations

Other Reflections

## Primary Qualities

At this moment in your career, what's your primary quality as a golfer? When asked to name a strength, some golfers identified the following:

| | | | | |
|---|---|---|---|---|
| Focused | Calm | Dedicated | Fit | Curious |
| Confident | Competitive | Motivated | Skillful | Easy-going |
| Leader | Unshakable | Positive | Strong | Creative |
| Hardworking | Fearless | Tenacious | Sociable | Graceful |

Write about your primary quality or strength...

# Playing Record

Date_____Course_____

Walk/Ride   Time Start_____End_____     Course Rating_____Slope_____Fees_____

Players/event: _____

Sleep_____Hydration before_____During_____

Nutrition before_____During_____

Weather_____

Warm-up_____

| Hole | Yards | My Par | Actual Strokes/Putts | + / - |
|------|-------|--------|----------------------|-------|
| 1    |       |        |                      |       |
| 2    |       |        |                      |       |
| 3    |       |        |                      |       |
| 4    |       |        |                      |       |
| 5    |       |        |                      |       |
| 6    |       |        |                      |       |
| 7    |       |        |                      |       |
| 8    |       |        |                      |       |
| 9    |       |        |                      |       |
| Out  |       |        |                      |       |
| 10   |       |        |                      |       |
| 11   |       |        |                      |       |
| 12   |       |        |                      |       |
| 13   |       |        |                      |       |
| 14   |       |        |                      |       |
| 15   |       |        |                      |       |
| 16   |       |        |                      |       |
| 17   |       |        |                      |       |
| 18   |       |        |                      |       |
| In   |       |        |                      |       |
| Total|       |        |                      |       |

Performance Observations

Other Reflections

## Proudest Moment

Other than winning a competition, tell the story of your proudest moment as a golfer. Why does this moment stand out? What do you take from it to inspire you?

# Playing Record

Date_____ Course_____

Walk/Ride   Time Start_____ End_____   Course Rating_____ Slope_____ Fees_____

Players/event: _____

Sleep_____ Hydration before_____ During_____

Nutrition before_____ During_____

Weather_____

Warm-up_____

| Hole | Yards | My Par | Actual Strokes/Putts | +/- |
|------|-------|--------|----------------------|-----|
| 1    |       |        |                      |     |
| 2    |       |        |                      |     |
| 3    |       |        |                      |     |
| 4    |       |        |                      |     |
| 5    |       |        |                      |     |
| 6    |       |        |                      |     |
| 7    |       |        |                      |     |
| 8    |       |        |                      |     |
| 9    |       |        |                      |     |
| Out  |       |        |                      |     |
| 10   |       |        |                      |     |
| 11   |       |        |                      |     |
| 12   |       |        |                      |     |
| 13   |       |        |                      |     |
| 14   |       |        |                      |     |
| 15   |       |        |                      |     |
| 16   |       |        |                      |     |
| 17   |       |        |                      |     |
| 18   |       |        |                      |     |
| In   |       |        |                      |     |
| Total|       |        |                      |     |

Performance Observations

Other Reflections

## Favorite Places 1

Write about the most appealing golf course (or hole) you have ever played. What makes it special?

# Playing Record

Date_____ Course_____

Walk/Ride   Time Start_____ End_____   Course Rating_____ Slope_____ Fees_____

Players/event: _____

Sleep_____ Hydration before_____ During_____

Nutrition before_____ During_____

Weather_____

Warm-up_____

| Hole | Yards | My Par | Actual Strokes/Putts | + / - |
|------|-------|--------|----------------------|-------|
| 1    |       |        |                      |       |
| 2    |       |        |                      |       |
| 3    |       |        |                      |       |
| 4    |       |        |                      |       |
| 5    |       |        |                      |       |
| 6    |       |        |                      |       |
| 7    |       |        |                      |       |
| 8    |       |        |                      |       |
| 9    |       |        |                      |       |
| Out  |       |        |                      |       |
| 10   |       |        |                      |       |
| 11   |       |        |                      |       |
| 12   |       |        |                      |       |
| 13   |       |        |                      |       |
| 14   |       |        |                      |       |
| 15   |       |        |                      |       |
| 16   |       |        |                      |       |
| 17   |       |        |                      |       |
| 18   |       |        |                      |       |
| In   |       |        |                      |       |
| Total|       |        |                      |       |

Performance Observations

Other Reflections

# Write about your favorite playing partner.

Name_____

Qualities as a golfer:

Qualities as a person:

Unique habits or quirks:

Best story about your playing partner:

What have you learned from this playing partner?

# Playing Record

Date_____Course_____

Walk/Ride   Time Start_____End_____        Course Rating_____Slope_____Fees_____

Players/event: _____

Sleep_____Hydration before_____During_____

Nutrition before_____During_____

Weather_____

Warm-up_____

| Hole | Yards | My Par | Actual Strokes/Putts | + / − |
|------|-------|--------|----------------------|-------|
| 1    |       |        |                      |       |
| 2    |       |        |                      |       |
| 3    |       |        |                      |       |
| 4    |       |        |                      |       |
| 5    |       |        |                      |       |
| 6    |       |        |                      |       |
| 7    |       |        |                      |       |
| 8    |       |        |                      |       |
| 9    |       |        |                      |       |
| Out  |       |        |                      |       |
| 10   |       |        |                      |       |
| 11   |       |        |                      |       |
| 12   |       |        |                      |       |
| 13   |       |        |                      |       |
| 14   |       |        |                      |       |
| 15   |       |        |                      |       |
| 16   |       |        |                      |       |
| 17   |       |        |                      |       |
| 18   |       |        |                      |       |
| In   |       |        |                      |       |
| Total|       |        |                      |       |

Performance Observations

Other Reflections

# Make Two Lists

During any round, golfers face a series of ups and downs that we have to manage to achieve consistent performance. How do you respond when things go well or not so well? When you sink that 30-foot putt, do you celebrate with a fist pump...or do you get so pumped up you hit a wild drive off the next tee? When you put one in the pond, do you grumble, "Man, I always do that," or do you simply say, "Huh, how unlike me," and focus on the next shot?

Make two lists: identify what you do when things go well and when they don't. For each item, try to plan how best to respond to keep your game on a steady track.

| What do you do when things go well? | What do you do when things don't go well? |
|---|---|
| | |

# Playing Record

Date_____Course_____

Walk/Ride   Time Start_____End_____   Course Rating_____ Slope_____Fees_____

Players/event: _____

Sleep_____Hydration before_____During_____

Nutrition before_____During_____

Weather_____

Warm-up_____

| Hole | Yards | My Par | Actual Strokes/Putts | + / - |
|------|-------|--------|----------------------|-------|
| 1    |       |        |                      |       |
| 2    |       |        |                      |       |
| 3    |       |        |                      |       |
| 4    |       |        |                      |       |
| 5    |       |        |                      |       |
| 6    |       |        |                      |       |
| 7    |       |        |                      |       |
| 8    |       |        |                      |       |
| 9    |       |        |                      |       |
| Out  |       |        |                      |       |
| 10   |       |        |                      |       |
| 11   |       |        |                      |       |
| 12   |       |        |                      |       |
| 13   |       |        |                      |       |
| 14   |       |        |                      |       |
| 15   |       |        |                      |       |
| 16   |       |        |                      |       |
| 17   |       |        |                      |       |
| 18   |       |        |                      |       |
| In   |       |        |                      |       |
| Total|       |        |                      |       |

Performance Observations

Other Reflections

## Getting Your Head on Straight

"The most controllable goal you can have is to hit every shot with total commitment, to go after it with a complete sense of purpose."

—Pia Nilsson & Lynn Marriott

Disruptions: In *Extraordinary Golf*, Fred Shoemaker talks about "self-interference," all those things we let into our head while trying to swing a golf club (e.g., Is my grip right? What are playing partners thinking? Will the wind gust now?). Parent calls these "anyways" as in, "I'm not focused and committed, but I'll go ahead and swing anyway" instead of stepping back and restarting my process.

Write about what tends to disrupt your concentration and how you respond to this interference and maintain your focus. On the course, keep track of those anyways. Here, describe what you become aware of and create plans for improving your concentration.

# Playing Record

Date_____Course_____

Walk/Ride  Time Start_____End_____    Course Rating_____Slope_____Fees_____

Players/event: _____

Sleep_____Hydration before_____During_____

Nutrition before_____During_____

Weather_____

Warm-up_____

| Hole | Yards | My Par | Actual Strokes/Putts | +/- |
|------|-------|--------|----------------------|-----|
| 1 | | | | |
| 2 | | | | |
| 3 | | | | |
| 4 | | | | |
| 5 | | | | |
| 6 | | | | |
| 7 | | | | |
| 8 | | | | |
| 9 | | | | |
| Out | | | | |
| 10 | | | | |
| 11 | | | | |
| 12 | | | | |
| 13 | | | | |
| 14 | | | | |
| 15 | | | | |
| 16 | | | | |
| 17 | | | | |
| 18 | | | | |
| In | | | | |
| Total | | | | |

Performance Observations

Other Reflections

# Reflection on Etiquette

"I never prayed that I would make a putt.
I prayed that I would react well if I missed."

— Chi Chi Rodriguez, World Golf Hall of Fame

We may not all be expert golfers, but we can all be expert at golf etiquette. Write about the behaviors that are important to you and the breaches in etiquette that bother you. How can you foster one and deal with the other?

# Playing Record

Date_____ Course_____

Walk/Ride  Time Start_____ End_____  Course Rating_____ Slope_____ Fees_____

Players/event: _____

Sleep_____ Hydration before_____ During_____

Nutrition before_____ During_____

Weather_____

Warm-up_____

| Hole | Yards | My Par | Actual Strokes/Putts | +/- |
|------|-------|--------|----------------------|-----|
| 1    |       |        |                      |     |
| 2    |       |        |                      |     |
| 3    |       |        |                      |     |
| 4    |       |        |                      |     |
| 5    |       |        |                      |     |
| 6    |       |        |                      |     |
| 7    |       |        |                      |     |
| 8    |       |        |                      |     |
| 9    |       |        |                      |     |
| Out  |       |        |                      |     |
| 10   |       |        |                      |     |
| 11   |       |        |                      |     |
| 12   |       |        |                      |     |
| 13   |       |        |                      |     |
| 14   |       |        |                      |     |
| 15   |       |        |                      |     |
| 16   |       |        |                      |     |
| 17   |       |        |                      |     |
| 18   |       |        |                      |     |
| In   |       |        |                      |     |
| Total|       |        |                      |     |

Performance Observations

Other Reflections

# Make Two Lists

In sports, there are things we can't control, like a bad bounce, and things we can, like how we react to it. Make a list of each, then write about a time when you let something you could *not* control get the better of you. What happened? How did you react? What would you do now under the same circumstances?

| Things I can control | Things I can't control |
|---|---|
| *Example: My pre-shot routine* | *Example: The weather* |

# Playing Record

Date_____Course_____

Walk/Ride   Time Start_____End_____    Course Rating_____Slope_____Fees_____

Players/event: _____

Sleep_____Hydration before_____During_____

Nutrition before_____During_____

Weather_____

Warm-up_____

| Hole | Yards | My Par | Actual Strokes/Putts | +/- |
|------|-------|--------|----------------------|-----|
| 1 | | | | |
| 2 | | | | |
| 3 | | | | |
| 4 | | | | |
| 5 | | | | |
| 6 | | | | |
| 7 | | | | |
| 8 | | | | |
| 9 | | | | |
| Out | | | | |
| 10 | | | | |
| 11 | | | | |
| 12 | | | | |
| 13 | | | | |
| 14 | | | | |
| 15 | | | | |
| 16 | | | | |
| 17 | | | | |
| 18 | | | | |
| In | | | | |
| Total | | | | |

Performance Observations

Other Reflections

## Who brings out your best and why?

Who brings out the best in you as a golfer and why? You might first think of an instructor or coach, playing partner or competitor. But also think about family members, friends, co-workers—those outside your golf orbit.

# Playing Record

Date_____ Course_____

Walk/Ride   Time Start_____ End_____   Course Rating_____ Slope_____ Fees_____

Players/event: _____

Sleep_____ Hydration before_____ During_____

Nutrition before_____ During_____

Weather_____

Warm-up_____

| Hole | Yards | My Par | Actual Strokes/Putts | +/- |
|------|-------|--------|----------------------|-----|
| 1    |       |        |                      |     |
| 2    |       |        |                      |     |
| 3    |       |        |                      |     |
| 4    |       |        |                      |     |
| 5    |       |        |                      |     |
| 6    |       |        |                      |     |
| 7    |       |        |                      |     |
| 8    |       |        |                      |     |
| 9    |       |        |                      |     |
| Out  |       |        |                      |     |
| 10   |       |        |                      |     |
| 11   |       |        |                      |     |
| 12   |       |        |                      |     |
| 13   |       |        |                      |     |
| 14   |       |        |                      |     |
| 15   |       |        |                      |     |
| 16   |       |        |                      |     |
| 17   |       |        |                      |     |
| 18   |       |        |                      |     |
| In   |       |        |                      |     |
| Total|       |        |                      |     |

Performance Observations

Other Reflections

# Performance Review: Ten Round Recap

Date:_____

Revisit records for the last ten rounds and reflect in the following areas.

| Round | Your Par | Your Actual |
|---|---|---|
|  |  |  |
|  |  |  |
|  |  |  |
|  |  |  |
|  |  |  |
|  |  |  |
|  |  |  |
|  |  |  |
|  |  |  |
|  |  |  |

*Readiness*: How prepared do you feel to play your best and enjoy each round: physically (sleep, nutrition, hydration), mentally and emotionally? What changes would you recommend?

*Performance*: Where are you gaining and losing strokes (i.e., scoring below or above your personal par on holes)? How do you know?

*Learning*: Where would you like to focus attention and what would you like to learn now?

*Enjoyment*: Where have you been experiencing joy in golf and how would you like to enhance the joy?

# Playing Record

Date_____Course_____

Walk/Ride   Time Start_____End_____   Course Rating_____Slope_____Fees_____

Players/event: _____

Sleep_____Hydration before_____During_____

Nutrition before_____During_____

Weather_____

Warm-up_____

| Hole | Yards | My Par | Actual Strokes/Putts | +/- |
|------|-------|--------|----------------------|-----|
| 1 | | | | |
| 2 | | | | |
| 3 | | | | |
| 4 | | | | |
| 5 | | | | |
| 6 | | | | |
| 7 | | | | |
| 8 | | | | |
| 9 | | | | |
| Out | | | | |
| 10 | | | | |
| 11 | | | | |
| 12 | | | | |
| 13 | | | | |
| 14 | | | | |
| 15 | | | | |
| 16 | | | | |
| 17 | | | | |
| 18 | | | | |
| In | | | | |
| Total | | | | |

Performance Observations

Other Reflections

# Learning to Adapt

Describe a course (or a hole) that you have learned to play differently over time—perhaps one that you once hated but have now come to love playing.

*Or Try This*: Describe a course (hole) that you play differently depending on conditions or the way you are playing on a particular day.

# Playing Record

Date_____Course_____

Walk/Ride   Time Start_____End_____   Course Rating_____Slope_____Fees_____

Players/event: _____

Sleep_____Hydration before_____During_____

Nutrition before_____During_____

Weather_____

Warm-up_____

| Hole | Yards | My Par | Actual Strokes/Putts | + / - |
|------|-------|--------|----------------------|-------|
| 1    |       |        |                      |       |
| 2    |       |        |                      |       |
| 3    |       |        |                      |       |
| 4    |       |        |                      |       |
| 5    |       |        |                      |       |
| 6    |       |        |                      |       |
| 7    |       |        |                      |       |
| 8    |       |        |                      |       |
| 9    |       |        |                      |       |
| Out  |       |        |                      |       |
| 10   |       |        |                      |       |
| 11   |       |        |                      |       |
| 12   |       |        |                      |       |
| 13   |       |        |                      |       |
| 14   |       |        |                      |       |
| 15   |       |        |                      |       |
| 16   |       |        |                      |       |
| 17   |       |        |                      |       |
| 18   |       |        |                      |       |
| In   |       |        |                      |       |
| Total|       |        |                      |       |

Performance Observations

Other Reflections

## See the Target (not the obstacle)

Self-fulfilling prophecy: Our mind naturally targets what we see. If we see the bunker instead of the green behind it, we tend to decelerate—landing in the sand instead of on the green. Write about hazards that draw your attention—and your ball. Then plan targets that can overpower those hazardous, mental images.

# Playing Record

Date_____ Course_____

Walk/Ride  Time Start_____ End_____  Course Rating_____ Slope_____ Fees_____

Players/event: _____

Sleep_____ Hydration before_____ During_____

Nutrition before_____ During_____

Weather_____

Warm-up_____

| Hole | Yards | My Par | Actual Strokes/Putts | +/- |
|------|-------|--------|----------------------|-----|
| 1    |       |        |                      |     |
| 2    |       |        |                      |     |
| 3    |       |        |                      |     |
| 4    |       |        |                      |     |
| 5    |       |        |                      |     |
| 6    |       |        |                      |     |
| 7    |       |        |                      |     |
| 8    |       |        |                      |     |
| 9    |       |        |                      |     |
| Out  |       |        |                      |     |
| 10   |       |        |                      |     |
| 11   |       |        |                      |     |
| 12   |       |        |                      |     |
| 13   |       |        |                      |     |
| 14   |       |        |                      |     |
| 15   |       |        |                      |     |
| 16   |       |        |                      |     |
| 17   |       |        |                      |     |
| 18   |       |        |                      |     |
| In   |       |        |                      |     |
| Total|       |        |                      |     |

Performance Observations

Other Reflections

"Do or do not. There is no try."
  –Yoda

What might these words from Jedi Master Yoda of *Star Wars* have to do with golf or other sports?

# Playing Record

Date_____ Course_____

Walk/Ride   Time Start_____ End_____   Course Rating_____ Slope_____ Fees_____

Players/event: _____

Sleep_____ Hydration before_____ During_____

Nutrition before_____ During_____

Weather_____

Warm-up_____

| Hole | Yards | My Par | Actual Strokes/Putts | + / - |
|------|-------|--------|----------------------|-------|
| 1    |       |        |                      |       |
| 2    |       |        |                      |       |
| 3    |       |        |                      |       |
| 4    |       |        |                      |       |
| 5    |       |        |                      |       |
| 6    |       |        |                      |       |
| 7    |       |        |                      |       |
| 8    |       |        |                      |       |
| 9    |       |        |                      |       |
| Out  |       |        |                      |       |
| 10   |       |        |                      |       |
| 11   |       |        |                      |       |
| 12   |       |        |                      |       |
| 13   |       |        |                      |       |
| 14   |       |        |                      |       |
| 15   |       |        |                      |       |
| 16   |       |        |                      |       |
| 17   |       |        |                      |       |
| 18   |       |        |                      |       |
| In   |       |        |                      |       |
| Total|       |        |                      |       |

Performance Observations

Other Reflections

## Favorite Places 2

Do you prefer easy or difficult courses? Write about your preference. Consider how the nature of the course affects each side of your triangle—performance, learning, and enjoyment.

# Playing Record

Date_____Course_____

Walk/Ride   Time Start_____End_____    Course Rating_____Slope_____Fees_____

Players/event: _____

Sleep_____Hydration before_____During_____

Nutrition before_____During_____

Weather_____

Warm-up_____

| Hole | Yards | My Par | Actual Strokes/Putts | +/- |
|------|-------|--------|----------------------|-----|
| 1    |       |        |                      |     |
| 2    |       |        |                      |     |
| 3    |       |        |                      |     |
| 4    |       |        |                      |     |
| 5    |       |        |                      |     |
| 6    |       |        |                      |     |
| 7    |       |        |                      |     |
| 8    |       |        |                      |     |
| 9    |       |        |                      |     |
| Out  |       |        |                      |     |
| 10   |       |        |                      |     |
| 11   |       |        |                      |     |
| 12   |       |        |                      |     |
| 13   |       |        |                      |     |
| 14   |       |        |                      |     |
| 15   |       |        |                      |     |
| 16   |       |        |                      |     |
| 17   |       |        |                      |     |
| 18   |       |        |                      |     |
| In   |       |        |                      |     |
| Total|       |        |                      |     |

Performance Observations

Other Reflections

## Changing the Conversation...Inside and Out

How we talk to others and ourselves can influence how we play. For example, the first tee is stressful and we're apt to hear (and say), "I haven't played for weeks," or "I'm trying a new grip," or "My back's been acting up again." These tend to lower our playing partners' expectations, but they can also lower the expectations we have for ourselves.

Write about ways you talk to others and yourself on the first tee, when facing hazards, or at other challenging times during a round. How could you speak more positively in ways that excite you for a challenge and boost confidence?

# Playing Record

Date_____ Course_____

Walk/Ride  Time Start_____ End_____   Course Rating_____ Slope_____ Fees_____

Players/event: _____

Sleep_____ Hydration before_____ During_____

Nutrition before_____ During_____

Weather_____

Warm-up_____

| Hole | Yards | My Par | Actual Strokes/Putts | +/- |
|---|---|---|---|---|
| 1 | | | | |
| 2 | | | | |
| 3 | | | | |
| 4 | | | | |
| 5 | | | | |
| 6 | | | | |
| 7 | | | | |
| 8 | | | | |
| 9 | | | | |
| Out | | | | |
| 10 | | | | |
| 11 | | | | |
| 12 | | | | |
| 13 | | | | |
| 14 | | | | |
| 15 | | | | |
| 16 | | | | |
| 17 | | | | |
| 18 | | | | |
| In | | | | |
| Total | | | | |

Performance Observations

Other Reflections

## Season Highlights

The funniest thing I've witnessed…

The happiest I've been…

The thing I thought but did not say to a playing partner…

The moment I wish I could take back…

# Playing Record

Date_____ Course_____

Walk/Ride   Time Start_____End_____        Course Rating_____ Slope_____ Fees_____

Players/event: _____

Sleep_____Hydration before_____During_____

Nutrition before_____During_____

Weather_____

Warm-up_____

| Hole | Yards | My Par | Actual Strokes/Putts | +/- |
|------|-------|--------|----------------------|-----|
| 1    |       |        |                      |     |
| 2    |       |        |                      |     |
| 3    |       |        |                      |     |
| 4    |       |        |                      |     |
| 5    |       |        |                      |     |
| 6    |       |        |                      |     |
| 7    |       |        |                      |     |
| 8    |       |        |                      |     |
| 9    |       |        |                      |     |
| Out  |       |        |                      |     |
| 10   |       |        |                      |     |
| 11   |       |        |                      |     |
| 12   |       |        |                      |     |
| 13   |       |        |                      |     |
| 14   |       |        |                      |     |
| 15   |       |        |                      |     |
| 16   |       |        |                      |     |
| 17   |       |        |                      |     |
| 18   |       |        |                      |     |
| In   |       |        |                      |     |
| Total|       |        |                      |     |

Performance Observations

Other Reflections

# Rapid Response

## Write about the following topics

Attitude

Managing Anxiety or Nervousness

Motivation

Handling Failure

Leveraging Success

# Playing Record

Date_____ Course_____

Walk/Ride   Time Start_____ End_____     Course Rating_____ Slope_____ Fees_____

Players/event: _____

Sleep_____ Hydration before_____ During_____

Nutrition before_____ During_____

Weather_____

Warm-up_____

| Hole | Yards | My Par | Actual Strokes/Putts | +/- |
|---|---|---|---|---|
| 1 | | | | |
| 2 | | | | |
| 3 | | | | |
| 4 | | | | |
| 5 | | | | |
| 6 | | | | |
| 7 | | | | |
| 8 | | | | |
| 9 | | | | |
| Out | | | | |
| 10 | | | | |
| 11 | | | | |
| 12 | | | | |
| 13 | | | | |
| 14 | | | | |
| 15 | | | | |
| 16 | | | | |
| 17 | | | | |
| 18 | | | | |
| In | | | | |
| Total | | | | |

Performance Observations

Other Reflections

# Trust

"A shot played with trust will get better results than one played with doubt. Doubt leads to confusion, anxiety, or both. Trust brings comfort and ease, and that allows you to let go and swing freely."

–Dr. Joseph Parent

How often have you driven an old, found ball instead of that $4 Titleist on a par-3 fronted by a water hazard? Confidence and trust—in our equipment, in our swing, in our decisions—is essential to carrying out our intentions as best we can. Write about fears that tend to disrupt your confidence and ways to combat or eliminate those fears.

# Playing Record

Date_____Course_____

Walk/Ride   Time Start_____End_____   Course Rating_____ Slope_____Fees_____

Players/event: _____

Sleep_____Hydration before_____During_____

Nutrition before_____During_____

Weather_____

Warm-up_____

| Hole | Yards | My Par | Actual Strokes/Putts | +/− |
|------|-------|--------|----------------------|-----|
| 1    |       |        |                      |     |
| 2    |       |        |                      |     |
| 3    |       |        |                      |     |
| 4    |       |        |                      |     |
| 5    |       |        |                      |     |
| 6    |       |        |                      |     |
| 7    |       |        |                      |     |
| 8    |       |        |                      |     |
| 9    |       |        |                      |     |
| Out  |       |        |                      |     |
| 10   |       |        |                      |     |
| 11   |       |        |                      |     |
| 12   |       |        |                      |     |
| 13   |       |        |                      |     |
| 14   |       |        |                      |     |
| 15   |       |        |                      |     |
| 16   |       |        |                      |     |
| 17   |       |        |                      |     |
| 18   |       |        |                      |     |
| In   |       |        |                      |     |
| Total|       |        |                      |     |

Performance Observations

Other Reflections

# Take a Fresh Look at the Landscape

In *Extraordinary Golf*, Shoemaker says, "Most of us play an incredibly boring game." We play familiar holes in the same way every time and respond to situations—distance and lie—in the same way with the same club.

Create: Take a hole you play often—and maybe not as well as you'd like—and design a new path from tee to hole (new targets, club selection...). Or, try this: design your path working backward from the hole to the tee.

Follow-up: Commit to taking this new path to the course.

# Playing Record

Date_____ Course_____

Walk/Ride   Time Start_____End_____   Course Rating_____ Slope_____ Fees_____

Players/event: _____

Sleep_____Hydration before_____During_____

Nutrition before_____During_____

Weather_____

Warm-up_____

| Hole | Yards | My Par | Actual Strokes/Putts | + / - |
|------|-------|--------|----------------------|-------|
| 1    |       |        |                      |       |
| 2    |       |        |                      |       |
| 3    |       |        |                      |       |
| 4    |       |        |                      |       |
| 5    |       |        |                      |       |
| 6    |       |        |                      |       |
| 7    |       |        |                      |       |
| 8    |       |        |                      |       |
| 9    |       |        |                      |       |
| Out  |       |        |                      |       |
| 10   |       |        |                      |       |
| 11   |       |        |                      |       |
| 12   |       |        |                      |       |
| 13   |       |        |                      |       |
| 14   |       |        |                      |       |
| 15   |       |        |                      |       |
| 16   |       |        |                      |       |
| 17   |       |        |                      |       |
| 18   |       |        |                      |       |
| In   |       |        |                      |       |
| Total|       |        |                      |       |

Performance Observations

Other Reflections

# Performance Review: Ready or Not

Some days before a round you feel "on." You're ready to have at it and everything is in sync. Some days... not so much. Why is that? What affects your performance? Food, friends, sleep, the opponent, work or school, your mood, or the wrong socks? Make two lists of what may influence your competitive performances, good and bad. Be as specific as you can about the influence.

| Good Round
Example: I feel rested. | Bad Round
Example: I lack confidence |
|---|---|
|  |  |
|  |  |
|  |  |
|  |  |
|  |  |
|  |  |
|  |  |
|  |  |

Write one or two sentences that capture your thinking about the lists above:

# Playing Record

Date_____ Course_____

Walk/Ride   Time Start_____ End_____   Course Rating_____ Slope_____ Fees_____

Players/event: _____

Sleep_____ Hydration before_____ During_____

Nutrition before_____ During_____

Weather_____

Warm-up_____

| Hole | Yards | My Par | Actual Strokes/Putts | +/- |
|------|-------|--------|----------------------|-----|
| 1 | | | | |
| 2 | | | | |
| 3 | | | | |
| 4 | | | | |
| 5 | | | | |
| 6 | | | | |
| 7 | | | | |
| 8 | | | | |
| 9 | | | | |
| Out | | | | |
| 10 | | | | |
| 11 | | | | |
| 12 | | | | |
| 13 | | | | |
| 14 | | | | |
| 15 | | | | |
| 16 | | | | |
| 17 | | | | |
| 18 | | | | |
| In | | | | |
| Total | | | | |

Performance Observations

Other Reflections

# Words of the Game

Watch golf on television and make a list of some of the announcer's best descriptive lines. What would you like to hear an announcer say during your round?

# Playing Record

Date_____Course_____

Walk/Ride   Time Start_____End_____   Course Rating_____Slope_____Fees_____

Players/event: _____

Sleep_____Hydration before_____During_____

Nutrition before_____During_____

Weather_____

Warm-up_____

| Hole | Yards | My Par | Actual Strokes/Putts | +/- |
|---|---|---|---|---|
| 1 | | | | |
| 2 | | | | |
| 3 | | | | |
| 4 | | | | |
| 5 | | | | |
| 6 | | | | |
| 7 | | | | |
| 8 | | | | |
| 9 | | | | |
| Out | | | | |
| 10 | | | | |
| 11 | | | | |
| 12 | | | | |
| 13 | | | | |
| 14 | | | | |
| 15 | | | | |
| 16 | | | | |
| 17 | | | | |
| 18 | | | | |
| In | | | | |
| Total | | | | |

Performance Observations

Other Reflections

# Rules Reflection

> "You might as well praise a man for not robbing a bank as to praise him for playing by the rules."
>
> —Bobby Jones

In recreational play, players take different positions on adhering to the rules of golf. Write a "position statement" for yourself on following the rules of golf, and reflect on how to handle players with a different point of view.

# Playing Record

Date_____ Course_____

Walk/Ride   Time Start_____ End_____      Course Rating_____ Slope_____ Fees_____

Players/event: _____

Sleep_____ Hydration before_____ During_____

Nutrition before_____ During_____

Weather_____

Warm-up_____

| Hole | Yards | My Par | Actual Strokes/Putts | +/- |
|------|-------|--------|----------------------|-----|
| 1    |       |        |                      |     |
| 2    |       |        |                      |     |
| 3    |       |        |                      |     |
| 4    |       |        |                      |     |
| 5    |       |        |                      |     |
| 6    |       |        |                      |     |
| 7    |       |        |                      |     |
| 8    |       |        |                      |     |
| 9    |       |        |                      |     |
| Out  |       |        |                      |     |
| 10   |       |        |                      |     |
| 11   |       |        |                      |     |
| 12   |       |        |                      |     |
| 13   |       |        |                      |     |
| 14   |       |        |                      |     |
| 15   |       |        |                      |     |
| 16   |       |        |                      |     |
| 17   |       |        |                      |     |
| 18   |       |        |                      |     |
| In   |       |        |                      |     |
| Total|       |        |                      |     |

Performance Observations

Other Reflections

# The Advantages of Doing Poorly

Why can this statement be true: "Some days, doing poorly is the most important result that could happen." Give examples from your own play as a golfer.

# Playing Record

Date_____ Course_____

Walk/Ride   Time Start_____ End_____   Course Rating_____ Slope_____ Fees_____

Players/event: _____

Sleep_____ Hydration before_____ During_____

Nutrition before_____ During_____

Weather_____

Warm-up_____

| Hole | Yards | My Par | Actual Strokes/Putts | +/- |
|------|-------|--------|----------------------|-----|
| 1    |       |        |                      |     |
| 2    |       |        |                      |     |
| 3    |       |        |                      |     |
| 4    |       |        |                      |     |
| 5    |       |        |                      |     |
| 6    |       |        |                      |     |
| 7    |       |        |                      |     |
| 8    |       |        |                      |     |
| 9    |       |        |                      |     |
| Out  |       |        |                      |     |
| 10   |       |        |                      |     |
| 11   |       |        |                      |     |
| 12   |       |        |                      |     |
| 13   |       |        |                      |     |
| 14   |       |        |                      |     |
| 15   |       |        |                      |     |
| 16   |       |        |                      |     |
| 17   |       |        |                      |     |
| 18   |       |        |                      |     |
| In   |       |        |                      |     |
| Total|       |        |                      |     |

Performance Observations

Other Reflections

# Are you getting enough sleep?

"Sleep is food for the brain."
                                         –The National Sleep Foundation

Go back through your workbook and add up the total hours of sleep you've had prior to rounds. Divide the total hours of sleep by the number of days you kept track.

Total Hours of Sleep _____ ÷ Number of Days _____ = _____ Average nightly hours of sleep before a round.

How does your sleep average compare with National Sleep Foundation recommendations?

| Ages | May Be Appropriate | Recommended | Not Recommended |
|---|---|---|---|
| 14-17 | 7 | 8-10 | 11 |
| 18-25 | 6 | 7-9 | 10 |
| 26-64 | 6 | 7-9 | 10 |
| 65 and older | 5-6 | 7-8 | 9 |

Write about your sleep habits and readiness to play.

# Playing Record

Date_____ Course_____

Walk/Ride   Time Start_____ End_____   Course Rating_____ Slope_____ Fees_____

Players/event: _____

Sleep_____ Hydration before_____ During_____

Nutrition before_____ During_____

Weather_____

Warm-up_____

| Hole | Yards | My Par | Actual Strokes/Putts | +/- |
|------|-------|--------|----------------------|-----|
| 1    |       |        |                      |     |
| 2    |       |        |                      |     |
| 3    |       |        |                      |     |
| 4    |       |        |                      |     |
| 5    |       |        |                      |     |
| 6    |       |        |                      |     |
| 7    |       |        |                      |     |
| 8    |       |        |                      |     |
| 9    |       |        |                      |     |
| Out  |       |        |                      |     |
| 10   |       |        |                      |     |
| 11   |       |        |                      |     |
| 12   |       |        |                      |     |
| 13   |       |        |                      |     |
| 14   |       |        |                      |     |
| 15   |       |        |                      |     |
| 16   |       |        |                      |     |
| 17   |       |        |                      |     |
| 18   |       |        |                      |     |
| In   |       |        |                      |     |
| Total|       |        |                      |     |

Performance Observations

Other Reflections

# Mental Imagery

Think back and recall your best moments in golf. Remember the exact details of a perfect pitch, brilliant strategy, or powerful drive. Make a list of those moments and create your own mental performance video that you can play back to yourself as preparation for a game or practice, or to use during a competition to gain back confidence. Your mental performance video might last between 10-30 seconds.

Example Image: A poor drive on the par-3 second leaves a downhill lie with water between my ball and the green. I select sand wedge, set the ball back in my stance, and *commit* to a crisp stroke *down* the slope, even if I end up in the rough behind the green. The beautiful result is one bounce and grab, stopping two feet from the cup.

Image:

Image:

Image:

Image:

Image:

# Playing Record

Date_____ Course_____

Walk/Ride   Time Start_____ End_____          Course Rating_____ Slope_____ Fees_____

Players/event: _____

Sleep_____ Hydration before_____ During_____

Nutrition before_____ During_____

Weather_____

Warm-up_____

| Hole | Yards | My Par | Actual Strokes/Putts | + / - |
|------|-------|--------|----------------------|-------|
| 1 | | | | |
| 2 | | | | |
| 3 | | | | |
| 4 | | | | |
| 5 | | | | |
| 6 | | | | |
| 7 | | | | |
| 8 | | | | |
| 9 | | | | |
| Out | | | | |
| 10 | | | | |
| 11 | | | | |
| 12 | | | | |
| 13 | | | | |
| 14 | | | | |
| 15 | | | | |
| 16 | | | | |
| 17 | | | | |
| 18 | | | | |
| In | | | | |
| Total | | | | |

Performance Observations

Other Reflections

# Grind Away

"Be prepared to scramble, right from the start."

—Jackie Burke, World Golf Hall of Fame

Bad shots tend to unravel us, and that can lead to a disappointing round and frustration. Commentators talk about "grinding" while professionals make the best of a round when they just don't have their A-game. It can be tough to trust ourselves—our swing or decision-making—but lack of confidence increases tension, and things can easily go from bad to worse. Write about the times you struggle and draft plans for grinding like a pro.

# Playing Record

Date_____ Course_____

Walk/Ride   Time Start_____ End_____     Course Rating_____ Slope_____ Fees_____

Players/event: _____

Sleep_____ Hydration before_____ During_____

Nutrition before_____ During_____

Weather_____

Warm-up_____

| Hole | Yards | My Par | Actual Strokes/Putts | +/- |
|------|-------|--------|----------------------|-----|
| 1    |       |        |                      |     |
| 2    |       |        |                      |     |
| 3    |       |        |                      |     |
| 4    |       |        |                      |     |
| 5    |       |        |                      |     |
| 6    |       |        |                      |     |
| 7    |       |        |                      |     |
| 8    |       |        |                      |     |
| 9    |       |        |                      |     |
| Out  |       |        |                      |     |
| 10   |       |        |                      |     |
| 11   |       |        |                      |     |
| 12   |       |        |                      |     |
| 13   |       |        |                      |     |
| 14   |       |        |                      |     |
| 15   |       |        |                      |     |
| 16   |       |        |                      |     |
| 17   |       |        |                      |     |
| 18   |       |        |                      |     |
| In   |       |        |                      |     |
| Total|       |        |                      |     |

Performance Observations

Other Reflections

## Favorite Movie

What's your favorite golf or sports movie and why? What do you like about the movie? Do you relate to any of the characters? Would you recommend this movie to a younger athlete? If so, why?

# Playing Record

Date_____ Course_____

Walk/Ride  Time Start_____ End_____  Course Rating_____ Slope_____ Fees_____

Players/event: _____

Sleep_____ Hydration before_____ During_____

Nutrition before_____ During_____

Weather_____

Warm-up_____

| Hole | Yards | My Par | Actual Strokes/Putts | + / - |
|------|-------|--------|----------------------|-------|
| 1    |       |        |                      |       |
| 2    |       |        |                      |       |
| 3    |       |        |                      |       |
| 4    |       |        |                      |       |
| 5    |       |        |                      |       |
| 6    |       |        |                      |       |
| 7    |       |        |                      |       |
| 8    |       |        |                      |       |
| 9    |       |        |                      |       |
| Out  |       |        |                      |       |
| 10   |       |        |                      |       |
| 11   |       |        |                      |       |
| 12   |       |        |                      |       |
| 13   |       |        |                      |       |
| 14   |       |        |                      |       |
| 15   |       |        |                      |       |
| 16   |       |        |                      |       |
| 17   |       |        |                      |       |
| 18   |       |        |                      |       |
| In   |       |        |                      |       |
| Total|       |        |                      |       |

Performance Observations

Other Reflections

## Your Choice

Select one or more of the terms on the left and write.

Good sport
Great eye
A good loss
Boundaries
Walking
Arnie
Injury
Fairway
Cheat
Focus
Jack
Fitness
Teammate
Official
Coach
Rough
Phil
Frightened
Technical
Discipline
Reward
Practice
Sand
St. Andrews
Distance
Wildlife
Break
Tiger
Etiquette
The Masters

# Playing Record

Date_____ Course_____

Walk/Ride  Time Start_____ End_____   Course Rating_____ Slope_____ Fees_____

Players/event: _____

Sleep_____ Hydration before_____ During_____

Nutrition before_____ During_____

Weather_____

Warm-up_____

| Hole | Yards | My Par | Actual Strokes/Putts | +/- |
|------|-------|--------|----------------------|-----|
| 1    |       |        |                      |     |
| 2    |       |        |                      |     |
| 3    |       |        |                      |     |
| 4    |       |        |                      |     |
| 5    |       |        |                      |     |
| 6    |       |        |                      |     |
| 7    |       |        |                      |     |
| 8    |       |        |                      |     |
| 9    |       |        |                      |     |
| Out  |       |        |                      |     |
| 10   |       |        |                      |     |
| 11   |       |        |                      |     |
| 12   |       |        |                      |     |
| 13   |       |        |                      |     |
| 14   |       |        |                      |     |
| 15   |       |        |                      |     |
| 16   |       |        |                      |     |
| 17   |       |        |                      |     |
| 18   |       |        |                      |     |
| In   |       |        |                      |     |
| Total|       |        |                      |     |

Performance Observations

Other Reflections

## Your Thoughtful Side

Write about a time this season when you were genuinely happy for another golfer's success, or tell about the kindest thing you have ever done as an athlete.

# Playing Record

Date_____ Course_____

Walk/Ride   Time Start_____ End_____   Course Rating_____ Slope_____ Fees_____

Players/event: _____

Sleep_____ Hydration before_____ During_____

Nutrition before_____ During_____

Weather_____

Warm-up_____

| Hole | Yards | My Par | Actual Strokes/Putts | + / - |
|------|-------|--------|----------------------|-------|
| 1 | | | | |
| 2 | | | | |
| 3 | | | | |
| 4 | | | | |
| 5 | | | | |
| 6 | | | | |
| 7 | | | | |
| 8 | | | | |
| 9 | | | | |
| Out | | | | |
| 10 | | | | |
| 11 | | | | |
| 12 | | | | |
| 13 | | | | |
| 14 | | | | |
| 15 | | | | |
| 16 | | | | |
| 17 | | | | |
| 18 | | | | |
| In | | | | |
| Total | | | | |

Performance Observations

Other Reflections

# Performance Review: Ten Round Recap

Date:_____

Revisit records for the last ten rounds and reflect in the following areas.

| Round | Your Par | Your Actual |
|---|---|---|
|  |  |  |
|  |  |  |
|  |  |  |
|  |  |  |
|  |  |  |
|  |  |  |
|  |  |  |
|  |  |  |
|  |  |  |
|  |  |  |

*Readiness*: How prepared do you feel to play your best and enjoy each round: physically (sleep, nutrition, hydration), mentally and emotionally? What changes would you recommend?

*Performance*: Where are you gaining and losing strokes (i.e., scoring below or above your personal par on holes)? How do you know?

*Learning*: Where would you like to focus attention and what would you like to learn now?

*Enjoyment*: Where have you been experiencing joy in golf and how would you like to enhance the joy?

# Playing Record

Date_____ Course_____

Walk/Ride   Time Start_____End_____   Course Rating_____ Slope_____ Fees_____

Players/event: _____

Sleep_____ Hydration before_____ During_____

Nutrition before_____ During_____

Weather_____

Warm-up_____

| Hole | Yards | My Par | Actual Strokes/Putts | +/- |
|------|-------|--------|----------------------|-----|
| 1    |       |        |                      |     |
| 2    |       |        |                      |     |
| 3    |       |        |                      |     |
| 4    |       |        |                      |     |
| 5    |       |        |                      |     |
| 6    |       |        |                      |     |
| 7    |       |        |                      |     |
| 8    |       |        |                      |     |
| 9    |       |        |                      |     |
| Out  |       |        |                      |     |
| 10   |       |        |                      |     |
| 11   |       |        |                      |     |
| 12   |       |        |                      |     |
| 13   |       |        |                      |     |
| 14   |       |        |                      |     |
| 15   |       |        |                      |     |
| 16   |       |        |                      |     |
| 17   |       |        |                      |     |
| 18   |       |        |                      |     |
| In   |       |        |                      |     |
| Total|       |        |                      |     |

Performance Observations

Other Reflections

# Stressed?

The American College of Sports Medicine listed the following signs and symptoms of stress in athletes.

| Behavioral | Physical | Psychological |
|---|---|---|
| Difficulty sleeping | Feeling ill | Negative self-talk |
| Lack of focus, overwhelmed | Cold, clammy hands | Inability to concentrate |
| Consistently performs better in practice/training than in competition | Profuse sweating | Uncontrollable intrusive and negative thoughts or images |
| Substance abuse | Headaches | Self doubt |
| | Increased muscle tension | |
| | Altered appetite | |

Referring to the chart above, write about your stress levels in each of the following areas:

Behavioral:



Physical:



Psychological:

# Playing Record

Date_____ Course_____

Walk/Ride  Time Start_____ End_____  Course Rating_____ Slope_____ Fees_____

Players/event: _____

Sleep_____ Hydration before_____ During_____

Nutrition before_____ During_____

Weather_____

Warm-up_____

| Hole | Yards | My Par | Actual Strokes/Putts | +/- |
|------|-------|--------|----------------------|-----|
| 1    |       |        |                      |     |
| 2    |       |        |                      |     |
| 3    |       |        |                      |     |
| 4    |       |        |                      |     |
| 5    |       |        |                      |     |
| 6    |       |        |                      |     |
| 7    |       |        |                      |     |
| 8    |       |        |                      |     |
| 9    |       |        |                      |     |
| Out  |       |        |                      |     |
| 10   |       |        |                      |     |
| 11   |       |        |                      |     |
| 12   |       |        |                      |     |
| 13   |       |        |                      |     |
| 14   |       |        |                      |     |
| 15   |       |        |                      |     |
| 16   |       |        |                      |     |
| 17   |       |        |                      |     |
| 18   |       |        |                      |     |
| In   |       |        |                      |     |
| Total|       |        |                      |     |

Performance Observations

Other Reflections

# Competition

Where, when, how, and with whom do you compete? Write about the benefits of competition.

# Playing Record

Date_____ Course_____

Walk/Ride   Time Start_____ End_____   Course Rating_____ Slope_____ Fees_____

Players/event: _____

Sleep_____ Hydration before_____ During_____

Nutrition before_____ During_____

Weather_____

Warm-up_____

| Hole | Yards | My Par | Actual Strokes/Putts | +/- |
|------|-------|--------|----------------------|-----|
| 1    |       |        |                      |     |
| 2    |       |        |                      |     |
| 3    |       |        |                      |     |
| 4    |       |        |                      |     |
| 5    |       |        |                      |     |
| 6    |       |        |                      |     |
| 7    |       |        |                      |     |
| 8    |       |        |                      |     |
| 9    |       |        |                      |     |
| Out  |       |        |                      |     |
| 10   |       |        |                      |     |
| 11   |       |        |                      |     |
| 12   |       |        |                      |     |
| 13   |       |        |                      |     |
| 14   |       |        |                      |     |
| 15   |       |        |                      |     |
| 16   |       |        |                      |     |
| 17   |       |        |                      |     |
| 18   |       |        |                      |     |
| In   |       |        |                      |     |
| Total|       |        |                      |     |

Performance Observations

Other Reflections

## Being Sponsored

How would your life as a golfer change if you had a sponsor who paid you $100,000 per year plus all of your expenses?

What if that sponsor placed the following condition on your sponsorship: If you do not land in the top 10% in all of your competitions in Year One, we will cut your sponsorship by half ($50,000). In Year Two, if you do not perform in the top 10% in each competition, we will drop the sponsorship by another half ($25,000). By Year Three, if you're not performing consistently in the top 10%, you will be dropped.

# Playing Record

Date_____ Course_____

Walk/Ride   Time Start_____ End_____    Course Rating_____ Slope_____ Fees_____

Players/event: _____

Sleep_____ Hydration before_____ During_____

Nutrition before_____ During_____

Weather_____

Warm-up_____

| Hole | Yards | My Par | Actual Strokes/Putts | +/- |
|------|-------|--------|----------------------|-----|
| 1    |       |        |                      |     |
| 2    |       |        |                      |     |
| 3    |       |        |                      |     |
| 4    |       |        |                      |     |
| 5    |       |        |                      |     |
| 6    |       |        |                      |     |
| 7    |       |        |                      |     |
| 8    |       |        |                      |     |
| 9    |       |        |                      |     |
| Out  |       |        |                      |     |
| 10   |       |        |                      |     |
| 11   |       |        |                      |     |
| 12   |       |        |                      |     |
| 13   |       |        |                      |     |
| 14   |       |        |                      |     |
| 15   |       |        |                      |     |
| 16   |       |        |                      |     |
| 17   |       |        |                      |     |
| 18   |       |        |                      |     |
| In   |       |        |                      |     |
| Total|       |        |                      |     |

Performance Observations

Other Reflections

> "Anger makes us stupid."
> —Pia Nilsson & Lynn Marriott

How often do we follow a poor shot with a stupid one? Or after running up a big number we look back and feel like a hole just flew by us? Write about when your mind has let you down and a hole has just gotten away from you. How can you see it coming...or happening...How can you put a stop to it?

# Playing Record

Date_____ Course_____

Walk/Ride   Time Start_____ End_____         Course Rating_____ Slope_____ Fees_____

Players/event: _____

Sleep_____ Hydration before_____ During_____

Nutrition before_____ During_____

Weather_____

Warm-up_____

| Hole | Yards | My Par | Actual Strokes/Putts | +/- |
|------|-------|--------|----------------------|-----|
| 1    |       |        |                      |     |
| 2    |       |        |                      |     |
| 3    |       |        |                      |     |
| 4    |       |        |                      |     |
| 5    |       |        |                      |     |
| 6    |       |        |                      |     |
| 7    |       |        |                      |     |
| 8    |       |        |                      |     |
| 9    |       |        |                      |     |
| Out  |       |        |                      |     |
| 10   |       |        |                      |     |
| 11   |       |        |                      |     |
| 12   |       |        |                      |     |
| 13   |       |        |                      |     |
| 14   |       |        |                      |     |
| 15   |       |        |                      |     |
| 16   |       |        |                      |     |
| 17   |       |        |                      |     |
| 18   |       |        |                      |     |
| In   |       |        |                      |     |
| Total|       |        |                      |     |

Performance Observations

Other Reflections

## Less is More

Henry David Thoreau wrote, "Less is more." Sometimes distilling our stories is a perfect way to see our athletic lives more clearly. Try to write some six-word sports stories about your play, practice sessions, or a recent round. For example, overcoming the challenge of a greenside bunker: "Trapped and short-sided—Splashed and Saved."

# Playing Record

Date_____ Course_____

Walk/Ride  Time Start_____ End_____    Course Rating_____ Slope_____ Fees_____

Players/event: _____

Sleep_____Hydration before_____During_____

Nutrition before_____During_____

Weather_____

Warm-up_____

| Hole | Yards | My Par | Actual Strokes/Putts | +/- |
|------|-------|--------|----------------------|-----|
| 1    |       |        |                      |     |
| 2    |       |        |                      |     |
| 3    |       |        |                      |     |
| 4    |       |        |                      |     |
| 5    |       |        |                      |     |
| 6    |       |        |                      |     |
| 7    |       |        |                      |     |
| 8    |       |        |                      |     |
| 9    |       |        |                      |     |
| Out  |       |        |                      |     |
| 10   |       |        |                      |     |
| 11   |       |        |                      |     |
| 12   |       |        |                      |     |
| 13   |       |        |                      |     |
| 14   |       |        |                      |     |
| 15   |       |        |                      |     |
| 16   |       |        |                      |     |
| 17   |       |        |                      |     |
| 18   |       |        |                      |     |
| In   |       |        |                      |     |
| Total|       |        |                      |     |

Performance Observations

Other Reflections

# Sports Psychology

Sports psychologists are a regular part of almost every professional golfer's team. Their work involves helping with issues like these:

|  |  |
|---|---|
| Mental preparedness | Goal setting |
| Managing anxiety | Reward strategies |
| Coping with stress | Visualization |
| Handling failure | Motivation |

If you're not familiar with some of these terms, do a quick online search. Now, page back through your reflections, round analyses, and practice session records and think how your writing in this notebook has helped you in any of these areas. Write.

# Playing Record

Date_____ Course_____

Walk/Ride   Time Start_____ End_____    Course Rating_____ Slope_____ Fees_____

Players/event: _____

Sleep_____ Hydration before_____ During_____

Nutrition before_____ During_____

Weather_____

Warm-up_____

| Hole | Yards | My Par | Actual Strokes/Putts | +/- |
|------|-------|--------|----------------------|-----|
| 1    |       |        |                      |     |
| 2    |       |        |                      |     |
| 3    |       |        |                      |     |
| 4    |       |        |                      |     |
| 5    |       |        |                      |     |
| 6    |       |        |                      |     |
| 7    |       |        |                      |     |
| 8    |       |        |                      |     |
| 9    |       |        |                      |     |
| Out  |       |        |                      |     |
| 10   |       |        |                      |     |
| 11   |       |        |                      |     |
| 12   |       |        |                      |     |
| 13   |       |        |                      |     |
| 14   |       |        |                      |     |
| 15   |       |        |                      |     |
| 16   |       |        |                      |     |
| 17   |       |        |                      |     |
| 18   |       |        |                      |     |
| In   |       |        |                      |     |
| Total|       |        |                      |     |

Performance Observations

Other Reflections

# Traditions

"Golf is a game of respect and sportsmanship;
we have to respect its traditions and its rules."

–Jack Nicklaus

Write about any aspect of the history and tradition of golf. What responsibility, if any, do you feel to the game and how do you preserve or pass that on?

# Playing Record

Date_____Course_____

Walk/Ride   Time Start_____End_____          Course Rating_____ Slope_____Fees_____

Players/event: _____

Sleep_____Hydration before_____During_____

Nutrition before_____During_____

Weather_____

Warm-up_____

| Hole | Yards | My Par | Actual Strokes/Putts | +/- |
|------|-------|--------|----------------------|-----|
| 1    |       |        |                      |     |
| 2    |       |        |                      |     |
| 3    |       |        |                      |     |
| 4    |       |        |                      |     |
| 5    |       |        |                      |     |
| 6    |       |        |                      |     |
| 7    |       |        |                      |     |
| 8    |       |        |                      |     |
| 9    |       |        |                      |     |
| Out  |       |        |                      |     |
| 10   |       |        |                      |     |
| 11   |       |        |                      |     |
| 12   |       |        |                      |     |
| 13   |       |        |                      |     |
| 14   |       |        |                      |     |
| 15   |       |        |                      |     |
| 16   |       |        |                      |     |
| 17   |       |        |                      |     |
| 18   |       |        |                      |     |
| In   |       |        |                      |     |
| Total|       |        |                      |     |

Performance Observations

Other Reflections

# Moments of the Season

Throughout a golfing season you experience highs and lows, ups and downs. Think back through the season and give quick examples of the following:

I laughed...

I cried or got emotional...

I wanted to hide...

I felt relieved...

I stood and stared in disbelief...

I just didn't care...

I got crazy angry...

I rejoiced...

# Playing Record

Date_____ Course_____

Walk/Ride   Time Start_____ End_____   Course Rating_____ Slope_____ Fees_____

Players/event: _____

Sleep_____ Hydration before_____ During_____

Nutrition before_____ During_____

Weather_____

Warm-up_____

| Hole | Yards | My Par | Actual Strokes/Putts | + / - |
|------|-------|--------|----------------------|-------|
| 1 | | | | |
| 2 | | | | |
| 3 | | | | |
| 4 | | | | |
| 5 | | | | |
| 6 | | | | |
| 7 | | | | |
| 8 | | | | |
| 9 | | | | |
| Out | | | | |
| 10 | | | | |
| 11 | | | | |
| 12 | | | | |
| 13 | | | | |
| 14 | | | | |
| 15 | | | | |
| 16 | | | | |
| 17 | | | | |
| 18 | | | | |
| In | | | | |
| Total | | | | |

Performance Observations

Other Reflections

# Why Write?

"Writing organizes and clarifies our thoughts. Writing is how we think our way into a subject and make it our own. Writing enables us to find out what we know—and what we don't know—about whatever we're trying to learn."

–William Zinsser, *Writing to Learn*

In what ways has this quotation proven true for you as a golfer who has kept a journal?

# Playing Record

Date_____ Course_____

Walk/Ride  Time Start_____ End_____   Course Rating_____ Slope_____ Fees_____

Players/event: _____

Sleep_____ Hydration before_____ During_____

Nutrition before_____ During_____

Weather_____

Warm-up_____

| Hole | Yards | My Par | Actual Strokes/Putts | +/- |
|------|-------|--------|----------------------|-----|
| 1    |       |        |                      |     |
| 2    |       |        |                      |     |
| 3    |       |        |                      |     |
| 4    |       |        |                      |     |
| 5    |       |        |                      |     |
| 6    |       |        |                      |     |
| 7    |       |        |                      |     |
| 8    |       |        |                      |     |
| 9    |       |        |                      |     |
| Out  |       |        |                      |     |
| 10   |       |        |                      |     |
| 11   |       |        |                      |     |
| 12   |       |        |                      |     |
| 13   |       |        |                      |     |
| 14   |       |        |                      |     |
| 15   |       |        |                      |     |
| 16   |       |        |                      |     |
| 17   |       |        |                      |     |
| 18   |       |        |                      |     |
| In   |       |        |                      |     |
| Total|       |        |                      |     |

Performance Observations

Other Reflections

# Retrospective

Go back through the words you've written in this notebook and make a list of your sentences, phrases, and words that are interesting, fun, introspective, and quirky about your season so far.

Notes:

# Practice Sessions

"Practice, which some regard as a chore,
should be approached as just about
the most pleasant recreation ever devised."

—Babe Didrikson Zaharias

# Practice Sessions

"The more I practice, the luckier I get."

—Gary Player

There are countless resources on what and how to practice in golf. Whatever program or advice you follow, this workbook can support thoughtful practice and awareness of what you do. Three guidelines will help:

*Practice must be interesting, even absorbing, if it is to be of any use* (Bobby Jones). Are you truly motivated to practice? If not, don't waste your time. Also, time warming up before a round—on the range or putting green—is not the time for practice. It's the time for a routine that launches your round in the most promising way.

*Have a defined purpose for any practice session.* Is it concentrated practice, where you are working to acquire or hone a particular skill or habit; or is it transfer practice in which you are working to take those skills to the course? One requires repetition while the other requires variation (changing your club and target between each stroke) as well as simulating play, for example, by going through your pre-shot routine with each stroke.

*You can learn more about the game on the practice area than anywhere else, and the higher your goal, the more time you spend there* (Arnold Palmer). What did you learn? Practice sessions deserve written reflection on results and next steps. The following pages can help you to plan before and review after each session and to reflect on how you learn and improve.

*Thinking of Making a Swing Change?*
A swing change can be a major undertaking. Ask yourself these questions, and write out an answer.

1. Where did you discover or hear about this change?
2. Why is it credible? Is it just the hottest new idea going around? Does it connect with an intention you already had for expanding your choices or overcoming a specific challenge? How high is it on your list of priorities?
3. How will this change affect your game? Identify how it will improve your game, but don't overlook how it might affect other parts of your game for better or worse.
4. Draft an actual plan for how you can try out the change and then, if you still like it, what you will need to do to make it part of your game.
    - Is this a plan you are willing to commit time and resources to? Are you prepared to suffer the inevitable decline in performance while making the change?
    - What support will you need? Who can you bounce your plan off?
5. Will this change make golf more fun for you?

# How to Use the Golfer's Practice Record

The Golfer's Practice Record (sample below) has space to record date & time, location, weather, and your readiness for each practice session—factors that may influence results. Beforehand: write a clear focus or purpose under "objective," and list each activity you plan to complete along with how long (and perhaps how many balls) you will use for each activity. The "comment" section may be used before or after to describe the activity purpose, mechanics, results, and so on. Finally, write a summary comment that describes results of the session and identifies future steps for practice.

## *Sample* Practice Record

Date/Time _June 1 (4:00)_     Location     _Meadow View – practice range_

Weather     _70° Sunny, Light wind (3-5 mph) crossing from left to right_

Readiness (sleep, nutrition & hydration, attitude): _After work so I felt a bit tired, drank plenty of water all day, ate granola and an orange before, feeling good about improvement with irons and ready to focus_

Objective: What is your main intention for today's practice session?
*Iron play: I've strengthened my grip and narrowed my stance on the course. Now I need to focus on whip-hand action–keep hands ahead of the clubface, delay uncocking my wrists, and whip the right hand through as the club turns over.*

| Duration | Activity | Comment |
|---|---|---|
| 15 minutes | *Warm-up: full stretch* | |
| (6 balls) | *Pitching wedges 50 yards* | *Check grip & stance, focus on rhythm.* |
| 20 minutes<br>(20 balls) | *8-iron: 130-140 yards* | *Concentrate on whip-hand action.* |
| 15 minutes<br>(16 balls) | *6-7-8-9 irons: Ladder up-and-down, vary distances and lies* | *Work on transferring whip-hand action to course conditions; observe distances.* |

Summary Comment: What went well, what did you learn, what are your next steps?

*Concentrated practice with the 8-iron improved accuracy and increased distance with that club (and also the nine, I think); seven- and especially six-iron was awful (hitting behind and turning over turf). Schedule concentrated practice with the six-iron.*

Every practice session must have a purpose.
"The key to more thoughtful golf is to expand your choices."
—Pia Nilsson & Lynn Marriott

Awareness (gathering information) and reflection (review empowered by writing) lead to learning and the opportunity for better, more enjoyable play. What choices would you like to add to your golfing arsenal? How can you begin to create or add those choices?

# Practice Record

Date/Time_____ Location_____

Weather_____

Readiness (sleep, nutrition & hydration, attitude):_____
_____

Objective: What is your main intention for today's practice session?

| Duration | Activity | Comment |
|---|---|---|
| | | |

Summary Comment: What went well, what did you learn, what are your next steps?

# What's in your bag?

List the things you carry on the course—clubs, ball markers, sunscreen, snacks, yardage book, range finder, and so on—and write short notes about each. (This is similar to the *Golf Digest* column on what pros carry in their bag.)

## Tools of the Trade

Write about your go-to club? How did it become your favorite? When, where, why do you rely on it?

What club(s) do you avoid? How does this handicap you? What can you do about that?

## Know Your Distances

A common trap we recreational golfers fall into is to make decisions based on our best shots instead of our average or most likely shots. If possible, find a range with clear yardage markers and work through your bag recording the distance on at least 5-6 shots with each club. (Remember not to take shots with any one club all in a row.) Record the average for each club on an index card, carry it with you on the course, and continue to fine-tune this guide. Here are some common averages for comparison.

| Club[1] | Average yardage men/women | | | My Distances | | | |
|---|---|---|---|---|---|---|---|
| | short | mid | long | | | | |
| PW | 80 / 50 | 105 / 60 | 120 / 80 | | | | |
| 9 Iron | 95 / 55 | 115 / 70 | 130 / 95 | | | | |
| 8 Iron | 110 / 60 | 130 / 80 | 140 / 110 | | | | |
| 7 Iron | 120 / 65 | 140 / 90 | 150 / 120 | | | | |
| 6 Iron | 130 / 70 | 150 / 100 | 160 / 130 | | | | |
| 5 Iron | 140 / 80 | 160 / 110 | 170 / 140 | | | | |
| 5 Hybrid[2] | 150 / 115 | 175 / 140 | 100 / 160 | | | | |
| 3 Hybrid[2] | 170 / 125 | 195 / 150 | 220 / 180 | | | | |
| 3 wood | 180 / 125 | 215 / 150 | 235 / 180 | | | | |
| Driver | 200 / 150 | 230 / 175 | 260 / 200 | | | | |

[1] Distance for irons, wood, and driver are from GolfLink.com.
[2] Distance for 3- and 5-hybrid are adapted from Golfweek.com.

## Practice Record

Date/Time_____Location_____

Weather_____

Readiness (sleep, nutrition & hydration, attitude):_____

_____

Objective: What is your main intention for today's practice session?

| Duration | Activity | Comment |
|----------|----------|---------|
|          |          |         |

Summary Comment: What went well, what did you learn, what are your next steps?

## Practice Record

Date/Time_____Location_____

Weather_____

Readiness (sleep, nutrition & hydration, attitude):_____

_____

Objective: What is your main intention for today's practice session?

| Duration | Activity | Comment |
|---|---|---|
| | | |

Summary Comment: What went well, what did you learn, what are your next steps?

# Training

What makes training hard for you?

What makes training easier for you?

## Practice Record

Date/Time_____ Location_____

Weather_____

Readiness (sleep, nutrition & hydration, attitude):_____

_____

Objective: What is your main intention for today's practice session?

| Duration | Activity | Comment |
|---|---|---|
|  |  |  |

Summary Comment: What went well, what did you learn, what are your next steps?

## Perfect Practice

Describe a perfect practice session. Where would it be? Who would attend? How long would it last? What activities would occur? Have you ever experienced perfection in a training session or practice? Write about that, too.

# Practice Record

Date/Time_____ Location_____

Weather_____

Readiness (sleep, nutrition & hydration, attitude):_____
_____

Objective: What is your main intention for today's practice session?

| Duration | Activity | Comment |
|---|---|---|
|  |  |  |

Summary Comment: What went well, what did you learn, what are your next steps?

# Get Out of Jail Cards

"Skill with recovery shots reduces fear with all shots."

—Dr. Joseph Parent

Identify recovery shots that would expand your choices when trouble comes calling. Draft a plan for acquiring each.

# Practice Record

Date/Time_____ Location_____

Weather_____

Readiness (sleep, nutrition & hydration, attitude):_____
_____

Objective: What is your main intention for today's practice session?

| Duration | Activity | Comment |
|---|---|---|
|  |  |  |

Summary Comment: What went well, what did you learn, what are your next steps?

# Practice Record

Date/Time_____Location_____

Weather_____

Readiness (sleep, nutrition & hydration, attitude):_____
_____

Objective: What is your main intention for today's practice session?

| Duration | Activity | Comment |
|---|---|---|
|  |  |  |

Summary Comment: What went well, what did you learn, what are your next steps?

# Practice Record

Date/Time_____ Location_____

Weather_____

Readiness (sleep, nutrition & hydration, attitude):_____
_____

Objective: What is your main intention for today's practice session?

| Duration | Activity | Comment |
|---|---|---|
|  |  |  |

Summary Comment: What went well, what did you learn, what are your next steps?

# Unpacking Your Training Days

Go back through the previous weeks of practice sessions, fill out the form below, and look closely at your results:

Number of practice sessions _____ What's your total practice time? _____

Typical Readiness (sleep, nutrition & hydration, attitude):

What have you done well during this period?

What do you think you need to improve upon?

Go back and read your "summary comments." Take a word or phrase from each session and place them below:

What does this list tell you about your training?

Revisit your practice session priorities for the season and write what you notice.

# Practice Record

Date/Time_____Location_____

Weather_____

Readiness (sleep, nutrition & hydration, attitude):_____
_____

Objective: What is your main intention for today's practice session?


| Duration | Activity | Comment |
|---|---|---|
|  |  |  |

Summary Comment: What went well, what did you learn, what are your next steps?

# Flip It

Most often, we approach the practice range with an intended goal in mind and a plan for how to work toward that goal. For a change, ask yourself, *I wonder what would happen if I [fill in the blank]*. In other words, list some variations in your swing or routine and see what results. For example, what if you close your stance, strengthen or weaken your grip, aim left or right, choke down on the club, don't take a practice swing, or even swing with your eyes closed?

# Practice Record

Date/Time_____ Location_____

Weather_____

Readiness (sleep, nutrition & hydration, attitude):_____
_____

Objective: What is your main intention for today's practice session?

| Duration | Activity | Comment |
|---|---|---|
|  |  |  |

Summary Comment: What went well, what did you learn, what are your next steps?

## Practice Record

Date/Time_____ Location_____

Weather_____

Readiness (sleep, nutrition & hydration, attitude):_____

_____

Objective: What is your main intention for today's practice session?

| Duration | Activity | Comment |
|---|---|---|
|  |  |  |

Summary Comment: What went well, what did you learn, what are your next steps?

# Practice Record

Date/Time_____ Location_____

Weather_____

Readiness (sleep, nutrition & hydration, attitude):_____
_____

Objective: What is your main intention for today's practice session?

| Duration | Activity | Comment |
|---|---|---|
|  |  |  |

Summary Comment: What went well, what did you learn, what are your next steps?

# Instructional Video

Think about one area that you'd like to improve upon. Use an Internet search engine like Google and find a video on that subject. Watch the video and write about the following:

Title of Video: _____

-What new information did you learn?

-What might you try out or how might you adapt to your game?

-What questions did you have after watching the video?

-What ideas might you share with a fellow golfer?

-What suggestions might you make for revising this video?

# Practice Record

Date/Time_____ Location_____

Weather_____

Readiness (sleep, nutrition & hydration, attitude):_____
_____

Objective: What is your main intention for today's practice session?

| Duration | Activity | Comment |
|---|---|---|
|   |   |   |

Summary Comment: What went well, what did you learn, what are your next steps?

# Practice Record

Date/Time_____ Location_____

Weather_____

Readiness (sleep, nutrition & hydration, attitude):_____
_____

Objective: What is your main intention for today's practice session?

| Duration | Activity | Comment |
|---|---|---|
|  |  |  |

Summary Comment: What went well, what did you learn, what are your next steps?

## Practice Record

Date/Time_____Location_____

Weather_____

Readiness (sleep, nutrition & hydration, attitude):_____

_____

Objective: What is your main intention for today's practice session?

| Duration | Activity | Comment |
|---|---|---|
|  |  |  |

Summary Comment: What went well, what did you learn, what are your next steps?

# Unpacking Your Training Days

Go back through the previous weeks of practice sessions, fill out the form below, and look closely at your results:

Number of practice sessions _____ What's your total practice time? _____

Typical Readiness (sleep, nutrition & hydration, attitude):


What have you done well during this period?


What do you think you need to improve upon?


Go back and read your "summary comments." Take a word or phrase from each session and place them below:




What does this list tell you about your training?




Revisit your practice session priorities for the season and write what you notice.

# Resource Bank

Throughout your time as a golfer, you have discovered some favorite resources that you've used to expand your knowledge and enjoyment. Make a list of some of the websites, YouTube videos, books, magazines, Facebook pages, or movies that you would recommend to a younger athlete.

Notes:

# Health and Fitness

Here's a place for you to reflect on your readiness to play. About every 8-10 rounds review your hydration, nutrition, and sleep records to identify trends that support or interfere with your performance. You may also plan any cross-training activities (e.g., treadmill, weights) and identify any injuries you may be managing.

# Your Readiness Review

Being healthy and fit is important in any sport. Search the Internet and you will discover endless recommendations for what to do and not do to be stronger and healthier, and play better golf.

This Readiness Review prepares you to play each round and make the most of each practice session. It is not about any specific exercise program to build strength or fitness.

Practice records and playing records for each round include space for three readiness factors: sleep, hydration, and nutrition. We recommend that you review these records after every 8-10 rounds or at the end of each month. Then, write two statements in each category:

- Summarize what you learned from your review.
- Draft a plan for future action.

Although it is not an exercise plan, the Readiness Review includes space to think about two other fitness categories:

- Cross-Training: What other fitness activities do you do on a regular basis? For example, you may walk on a treadmill each day, follow a weight-lifting program, or participate in a yoga class.
- Injury Management: Have you been dealing with any chronic issues like lower back pain or hip flexor stiffness? How about temporary injuries like blisters on your hands or feet?

You might use the *Other Notes* section (p. 173) of this workbook to write in more detail about these conditions and how you are managing them. Use the Readiness Review for brief statements about your current status and future plans for each.

Finally, remember that physical warm-up before a round or practice session is perhaps the most important part of readiness to play. Properly performed stretches not only increase power and range of motion, they are also essential to avoiding injuries that recreational golfers too often develop. Each readiness review is a good time to check your warm-up routine and playing records to be sure you are taking your warm-up time seriously.

Page 159 (opposite) is a sample Readiness Review with typical statements in each category.

# Readiness Review

Date: __June 5th__

I have reviewed my playing and practice records from __May 1__ to __June 1__.

| Review Statement | Planning Statement |
|---|---|
| **Sleep** | |
| I don't see any patterns in sleep affecting my play, but I don't seem to play as well when rounds start right after lunch (between 12-2). | I might monitor this to see if it's a pattern. |
| **Hydration** | |
| I have played better when I drink at least 12 ounces of water during a round. | I will put a star on my scorecard after every three holes to remind me to take a drink. |
| **Nutrition** | |
| What I eat during rounds is inconsistent. | Commit to eating at least one fruit and one nut/granola mix during each round. |
| **Cross-Training Activities** | |
| Now that I'm playing again, I'm not walking on the treadmill like I did in the off-season. | I should at least commit to walking 20 minutes, twice a day when I don't play golf. |
| **Injuries** | |
| I'm still experiencing occasional blisters on my right instep. | I need to put some moleskin in my golf bag and use as needed. I might investigate if this has something to do with my shoes or my swing. |

Are you warming up before each round? If not, why not and what can you do about that?

> I'm definitely stretching and putting before each round. I haven't usually been hitting at the range though. I really don't want to take the time for a whole bucket. Maybe I can split a bucket with someone in my foursome and hit 12-15 balls before each round.

# Readiness Review

Date:

I have reviewed my playing and practice records from _____ to _____.

| Review Statement | Planning Statement |
|---|---|//

Sleep




Hydration




Nutrition




Cross-Training Activities




Injuries




Are you warming up before each round? If not, why not and what can you do about that?

# Readiness Review

Date:

I have reviewed my playing and practice records from _____ to _____.

| Review Statement | Planning Statement |
|---|---|
| Sleep | |
| Hydration | |
| Nutrition | |
| Cross-Training Activities | |
| Injuries | |

Are you warming up before each round? If not, why not and what can you do about that?

# Readiness Review

Date:

I have reviewed my playing and practice records from_____ to _____.

| Review Statement | Planning Statement |
|---|---|
| Sleep | |
| Hydration | |
| Nutrition | |
| Cross-Training Activities | |
| Injuries | |

Are you warming up before each round? If not, why not and what can you do about that?

# Readiness Review

Date:

I have reviewed my playing and practice records from _____ to _____.

| Review Statement | Planning Statement |
|---|---|
| Sleep | |
| Hydration | |
| Nutrition | |
| Cross-Training Activities | |
| Injuries | |

Are you warming up before each round? If not, why not and what can you do about that?

# Readiness Review

Date:

I have reviewed my playing and practice records from_____ to _____.

| Review Statement | Planning Statement |
|---|---|
| Sleep | |
| Hydration | |
| Nutrition | |
| Cross-Training Activities | |
| Injuries | |

Are you warming up before each round? If not, why not and what can you do about that?

Notes:

# Additional Writing Activities

Here are an additional 15 prompts for those who have fallen in love with writing. There's also space to describe your fantasy golf foursome and to plan your dream golfing trip.

# Additional Writing Activities

Use the space provided or the *Other Notes* section (p. 171) of this workbook to write about these topics.

1. *Failure*

    Professor Dan Gerdes asked his sports psychology students to explore how failure can be helpful. Among the list his students compiled were the following—write about them:

    *Failure found what didn't work.*
    *Failure creates hunger to do better.*
    *Failure adds value to success.*
    *Failure is feedback.*

2. Describe your greatest disappointment as a golfer thus far in your career. What did you learn from the experience?

3. Have you ever been dishonest in golf? If so, why? What did you learn from this experience? If you haven't been dishonest or don't want to write about it, have you witnessed dishonesty on the part of another golfer? If so, how did it make you feel?

4. Write about this quotation from Boston Marathon winner Amby Burfoot: "To get to the finish line, you'll have to try lots of different paths."

5. Describe what it's like to hit "the wall" during training or a competition.

6. If you could relive one moment as a golfer, what would it be and why would you want to go back?

7. What is a good opponent?

8. What advice or talk do you *least* like to hear before an important match and why?

9. List five (or more) qualities that describe your golf swing (not its results, but the swing itself). Then, list some qualities you would like to see in your swing. Draft some affirmations or plans for trying one or more of these qualities at the practice range.

10. How would you like others to describe you as a competitor?

11. At this moment in your career, what's your primary weakness as a golfer? When asked to name a weakness, some athletes identified these:

| | | | |
|---|---|---|---|
| Nervous | Insecure | Frightened | Weak |
| Timid | Unreliable | Unhealthy | Unfocused |
| Hot-tempered | Unfocused | Lazy | Disorganized |
| Know-it-all | Negative | Whiner | Inconsistent |

Write about your primary weakness and what you plan to do to correct this challenge.

12. What would you do differently if you could have a "do-over" in your last match or competition?

13. Making Meaning Activity: *Training*

    *Step #1:* List some of the words that come to mind when you think about "training." Place the words in the chart below.

    *Step #2:* Name the opposite of the words in Step One. Looking at both sides of any topic (i.e., true/false, positive/negative, right/wrong) can help us come to know a topic more fully.

    | Step #1<br>Example: easy | Step #2<br>Example: hard |
    |---|---|
    | | |

    *Step #3:* Write two sentences about training using two pair of the opposing words from above. For example: *Some days training is <u>easy</u> because I feel strong; other days training is <u>difficult</u>, and I feel like I'm going backwards and getting weaker.*

    *Step #4:* Write a 5-sentence paragraph about <u>training</u> using the guidelines below. This exercise will help you find your "truth" about training.

    Sentence 1  a five-word statement
    Sentence 2  a question
    Sentence 3  two independent clauses combined by a semi-colon
    Sentence 4  a sentence with an introductory phrase
    Sentence 5  a two-word statement

14. Describe your fantasy foursome of golfers (living or not, personal or professional) and describe how you imagine the day.

15. Plan your dream golf trip.

# Appendix: Creating a Personal Par

*How to calculate an unofficial handicap index*

This is *not* the complete method for calculating a handicap differential. You can easily find more detailed information online. In the meantime, this will give you a working number.

Take the average total score of ten rounds from your home course (the ten best out of 20 rounds is better, but if you're just starting out and don't have either number, just use whatever you know is an honest average score for 18 holes at your home course).

You'll also need the "course rating" and "slope rating" from your home course. These numbers should be on the course scorecard. Then, here's the math:

(your average score - the course rating) x (113/slope rating) = # x 0.96 = Your Handicap "Index."

For example, your average is 22 over par at your home course which is a par-70 course with a course rating of 65.6 and a slope rating of 102: Handicap Index: (92 - 65.6) x (113/102) = 29.3 x 0.96 = 28.1. Therefore, you should take one added stroke on each hole plus 10 more strokes distributed across the 18 holes.

If you calculated your index using an average of scores from your home course only, then that index is also your handicap at your home course. When you travel to other courses, you will need to calculate a number for those courses. Here's how:

(Your Handicap index) x (slope rating from the course you are playing / 113). Using the above example, if you play a course with a slope rating of 119: (28.1) x (119/113) = 29.6.

*How to fine-tune your personal par plan*

The USGA way to determine where to add or subtract strokes and fine-tune your personal par plan: Course scorecards mark where "handicap strokes" are taken in competition. The number "1" handicap stroke is taken at the most difficult hole, number "2" at the second most difficult, and so on down to number "18" which is the least difficult hole. When deciding where to add strokes, begin with #1 (the most difficult hole on the course); and when deciding where not to take additional strokes, begin with #18 (the easiest handicap hole).

In the example above, you would take one stroke on each of the 18 holes on the course. Then you would take 10 more strokes: one stroke added to the $1^{st}$ (most difficult) handicap hole, one to the $2^{nd}$ handicap hole…down to a $10^{th}$ stroke at the $10^{th}$ handicap hole.

# Other Notes

The following pages provide room for whatever doesn't fit anywhere else. This section includes graph paper for sketching and planning strategy for holes you play or perhaps for designing your own ideal golf holes.

NOTES_____ DATE_____

NOTES_____  DATE_____

_____
_____
_____
_____
_____
_____
_____

Continue writing or use this box to doodle or sketch ideas.

NOTES_____ DATE_____

NOTES_____  DATE_____

_____
_____
_____
_____
_____
_____
_____

Use this graph to sketch ways of attacking a golf hole or your own design for a hole.

NOTES_____ DATE_____

NOTES_____ DATE_____

Continue writing or use this box to doodle or sketch ideas.

NOTES_____  DATE_____

NOTES_____  DATE_____

Use this graph to sketch ways of attacking a golf hole or your own design for a hole.

NOTES_____ DATE_____

NOTES_____  DATE_____

_____
_____
_____
_____
_____
_____
_____

Continue writing or use this box to doodle or sketch ideas.

NOTES_____    DATE_____

NOTES_____ DATE_____

Use this graph to sketch ways of attacking a golf hole or your own design for a hole.

NOTES_____  DATE_____

NOTES_____  DATE_____

_____
_____
_____
_____
_____
_____
_____
_____

Continue writing or use this box to doodle or sketch ideas.

NOTES_____  DATE_____

NOTES_____ DATE_____

Use this graph to sketch ways of attacking a golf hole or your own design for a hole.

NOTES_____ DATE_____

NOTES_____  DATE_____

_____
_____
_____
_____
_____
_____
_____

Continue writing or use this box to doodle or sketch ideas.

NOTES_____    DATE_____

NOTES_____ DATE_____

Use this graph to sketch ways of attacking a golf hole or your own design for a hole.

# About the Authors

*Ken Martin & Richard Kent*

RICHARD KENT is a professor at the University of Maine and director emeritus of the Maine Writing Project, a site of the National Writing Project. He is the author of many books, including *Writing on the Bus*, *The Athlete's Workbook*, and *VO$_2$ Max Athlete's Journal*, and maintains a resource website at WritingAthletes.com. A coach for 39 years, Rich can be found most afternoons hiking, running, or cross-country skiing the mountains of western Maine with Bailey Tuckerman, his Bernese Mountain Dog.

KEN MARTIN first played golf as a boy at Cohasset Country Club, a parkland course in Massachusetts where he also caddied. As a high school teacher and track & field and cross-country coach, he realized how powerful writing could be in support of learning and improving his own game. As Director of the Maine Writing Project and a literacy professor at the University of Maine, Ken continued his focus on the interconnection of writing and learning, extended here to performance in golf.

*Write. Learn. Perform.*

www.ingramcontent.com/pod-product-compliance
Lightning Source LLC
Chambersburg PA
CBHW081456040426
42446CB00016B/3262